Gloria Pitzer's Copycat Cookbook

Dear Friends

SINCE 1973 we've made Secret Recipes the simple

THE INSIDE STORY

IN THIS BOOK I will draw a parallel between most of the recipe secrets I share with you here, and those dishes we have always enjoyed while eating out, or which we have purchased from the supermarket.

SIMPLE REPRODUCTIONS of both restaurant food and grocery store products can be so helpful to the cook who wants salvation from suffering over a hot stove all day! Never mind the critics! They'll clamour for their well-deserved attention, no matter what we prefer. Critics are paid to find fault. They don't care about you and they don't care about me. They care about being right! They care about keeping their jobs. Although most of the time they cannot prove that they are right in their righteousness, they can enlist the support of a dubious public, long enough to sway opinion in the direction in which t-h-e-y—the critics—wish it to go.

IF YOU LIKE TO IMITATE FAMOUS FOODS in your own kitchen, open your file box everytime you're at a loss for what to prepare for your table and try to reproduce your favorite dishes with enthusiasm and with a caring attitude that you can make mealtime more meaningful than it ever was portrayed in the classic cookbooks. We, as a society, seem to listen too much to those who insist we be more original, that we concentrate more on nutrition and health. They prey on our conscience with statistics of starvation and malnutrition. The one thing I would not presume to do in my conversations with you about foods and restaurants, is to assume that because I like something that you will, too! You have choices to make and all I can do is recommend a dish, or a restaurant on the basis that it compares favorably to another food or restaurant with which we are familiar. In a society of people who live by the "don't get me involved" principle where simple human relationships are concerned, how can we put our trust and faith in the evangelists of the food industry to know for certain if what they insist is wrong, or bad for us, or dangerous, really IS!

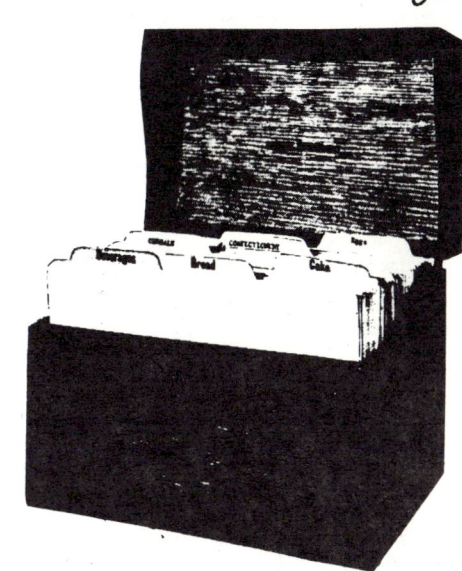

Reproductions
Copycat
Recipes

to recreate in your own home, customized to your needs.

A world of good cooking

In February of 1988 when Paul and I went to Los Angeles to present some of our recipes on The Home Show, with Rob Weller and Sandy Hill, I knew that another book was eminent. At that show, prior to the filming, I was in what they refer to as the "backstage kitchen" trying to repair two of the recipes their cooks were to have prepared for me from my own recipes to present on television. These professional cooks had trouble with the results and I had to find out w-h-y. What I learned prompted me to put together enough helpful information and new recipes that we just had to do another book.

Some useful information

THE FUNDAMENTALS

When I saw that the cookies prepared by the staff cooks had burned and were not at all like mine, even b-e-f-o-r-e they were baked, I had them show me exactly what they did. They insisted they followed my recipe to the letter. But I knew they thought they did, when in fact, they had overlooked something that caused the problem. The same could happen to the cook at home in their own kitchen, going through my books for the first time and having the results turn out less than perfectly! I discovered the only measuring cup handy at that backstage kitchen was a 2-cup Pyrex measuring cup. This is for liquid measuring only, but apparently was used to measure the Bisquick used in the biscuit recipe in which the dough turned out like a glob of cement! In using that cup, rather than a metal measuring cup, designed for dry ingredients, they actually ended up with 2½-cups Bisquick, rather than the 2 cups called for. They also used silverware teaspoons to measure the other ingredients that required measuring teaspoons and this produced almost twice the amount required. The cookies, I learned burned because they did not have a cookie sheet but used a jelly roll pan instead, that was, in fact, exactly the same dimension as the inside of the oven, so to get it to fit, they had to force it onto the top rack of the oven in order to also be able to close the oven door. I was able to remedy the situation in preparing a second batch of cookies, by covering the broiler pan rack in foil and using that as a cookie sheet, placing it on the c-e-n-t-e-r rack of the oven, where 90% of all cookies will be baked, unless a recipe otherwise specifies another position.

When the jelly roll pan was forced to fit into the oven on the top rack, what happened, was the heat from the oven floor had no where to go but straight up and was stopped by the bottom of the pan. The heat should have been able to circulate around the pan on all 4 sides, equally distanced from each of the 4 sides of the oven. This is important to adequate baking of any oven dish — seeing to it that the heat circulated around the food! Other possible drawbacks to why recipes don't always turn out exactly as promised will be covered here and there through this collection. If a pie crust is tough, a meringue deflates and weeps, a loaf of bread is dry of has holes in it, how to thicken up soupy baked beans, keep biscuits light and tender, and dozens of others.

©1993 by Gloria Pitzer. All rights reserved. No part of this publication may be reproduced or transmitted in any form or by any means, mechanical or electronic, including photocopying, recording, or by any information storage and retrieval system, without permission in writing from Gloria Pitzer. Not for resale. Published by Secret Recipes Box 237, Marysville, MI 48040. Sold by mail. Canadian orders please use U.S. funds. Mailed via First Class Postage to all subscribers. Printed in U.S.A.

I know I said I would never do a another national television show after the Donahue experience (July 1981), but when good friend, Carol Duval, called me and asked me to give the Home Show a try, I was glad that I finally agreed. The most exciting part of the experience was being completely surprised by a visit on stage from Wally Amos, who, in 1975 founded the world's first cookie shop. The Home Show had brought him into Los Angeles just to meet me and sample my version of his product, which I was preparing on that show. I was absolutely delighted with the sample tin of his assorted cookies, which because of the small size, I call "little love bumps". In my BETTER COOKERY Cookbook I give you accounts of unhappy experiences with companies whose legal advisers had us quite frightened at one time, for having attempted to duplicate their secrets in my own kitchen. Wally Amos, like Harland Sanders, Jack Sanders (not of KFC, but of the famous confectionary), along with Arthur Treacher, the people at White Castle Hamburgers and those good folks at General Foods, as well as McDonalds own Paul Duncan, have given me encouragement, as well as appreciation for having attempted to compliment them with flattery.

I still, however, do prefer the wonders of radio to that of doing television presentations. My favorite contacts are always with radio listeners, because it is a more personal communication, like friends or family, where television is a vast make-believe land of 90% cosmetic appearance. The imagination can be free to explore new ideas more readily with radio, I believe. No matter what time of the day or night — and often that means the middle of the night, too — the broadcasts are always lively and interesting and include challenging questions and requests from enthusiastic listeners.

Because we do not have our books in bookstores, sending them out o-n-l-y by mail, from our address, we have been able to acquaint many folks with our work by talking about the secrets of the food industry over the radio. From California to New York, From Florida, Texas, Oklahoma and then as far north as Washington State and into Canada, we have visited with listeners. We've talked to folks in Japan and Australia, Guam, Hawaii, even Alaska, as well as West Germany — and we've confirmed what Walt Disney knew all along — it's a small, small world, afterall. Making new friends through good food ideas, we've helped to take the monotony out of mealtime and turn a job into a joy!

CONFESSIONS OF A CLOSET GOURMET

I HAVE ALWAYS BEEN just slightly intimidated by exceptionally good cooks who don't hesitate for a minute to confess with candor, how splendid they are in the culinary arts. I suppose I would be proud to admit without prompting, that I, too, was an exceptional cook, had I been as fortunate in fixing foods that had favorable results. But, alas, I still maintain that if the Good Lord had intended for me to be a gourmet cook, I would have been born with Teflon hands! There are, however, many more things I would rather do than hang around the kitchen all day, stirring a creative concoction that will be gobbled down in much less time than it took me to shop for the ingredients, tote them home, prepare the recipes, and finally present the dishes with those who share my table with me.

NO MATTER HOW MANY OFFERS Paul & I have had from New York publishers to take over our recipes for us, I could not bring myself to this in any agreement, because they would immediately try to make my books look like, read like and compete with all of the other cookbooks on the market. I don't think of other cookbooks as being "competition"—but as "companions" in the kitchen. My competition is not in the cookbook field, but in the commercial food industry, where I can sleuth out the secrets of making at home, what we can buy in the marketplace—when we can afford it—without even knowing what they put into their products. The writer Coulton said that Imitation is the sincerest form of flattery—and I add—also the sincerest form of competition, as so well proven by McDonald's, Wendy's, Burger King and the hundreds of other participants in the fast food industry.

Talking Food

AN HONEST REPORT

COMPANY'S COMING

A Successful Prescription
CHURCH PARLOR PUNCH

This is probably the best non-alcoholic party punch you will ever enjoy! When Paul and I were married in June of 1956, we had our wedding dinner at Devon Gables, a restaurant in Bloomfield Hills (Mich), which years ago burned down. I am so glad that I kept this recipe for it is almost exactly like the punch served at our wedding dinner!

STRAWBERRY

1 package Daquiri Mix powder
   (a non-alcoholic mix sold at liquor counters)
2 pkgs (10-oz each) sliced sweetened strawberries
1-quart "red pop" (strawberry or cherry flavored soda)
2-qts Canada Dry Gingerale
2 trays (about 40) ice cubes

Combine Daquiri Mix powder with slightly thawed strawberries, mashing this together with pastry blender or potato masher, till thoroughly combined. Add the carbonated beverages and ice cubes and serve satisfactorily to 12 who want "seconds" in 6-oz glasses or to 15 in little punch cups.

Not recommended for sugar-free diets.

Gloria Pitzer's Copycat Cookbook — Pages 5 & 6

CINCINNATI CHILI (Served 5 Ways!)

Brown 2-lbs ground beef in a little oil in large skillet, crumbling beef with fork till pink color disappear, medium high heat. Put ½-cup Cola & 1 cup of meat into blender, high speed, till it's the consistency of cement mortar! Return blender mixture to rest of meat & add to it—1 envelope onion soup mix, 1-lb jar Prego Spaghetti Sauce, 1 TB chili powder, 1½-tsp cumin powder, ½-tsp allspice, 2 TB chocolate syrup, 8-oz Cola. Heat on low, uncovered 1 hr. Spoon sauce over grilled hot dogs in buns or serve it 4 other ways: with spaghetti, with beans, with shredded Cheddar cheese, with chopped onions, as they do in the Cincinnati Chili parlors.

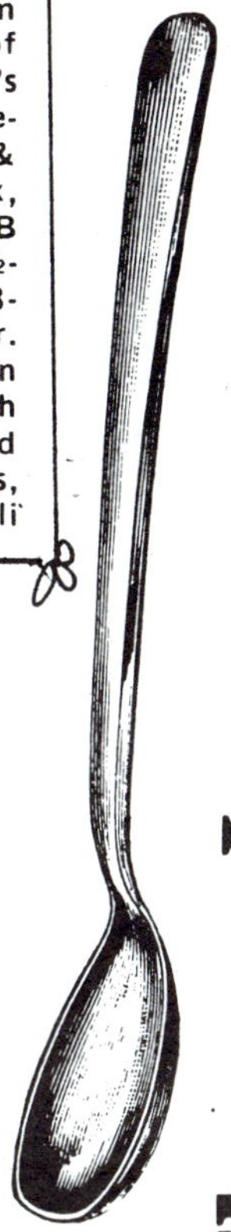

CHILI RECIPES, especially in restaurants, vary greatly according to regional influences. In the Midwest, Chili has a rich tomato-y base. In California, Chili is more like a Michigan Sloppy Joe mixture. In Texas, Chili is spicy and hot. In New York, Chili is "con carne", with beans, and usually a thick-soup like mixture which sets it apart from the famous Coney Island Sauce. Coney Sauce is spooned over hot dogs in buns, or served without hot dogs, in buns, topped off with fresh chopped onions or shredded Cheddar. Greek Coney Island Sauce is always accentuated with ground cumin and Chili powder. The ratio of these 2 spices is generally half as much cumin as Chili powder.

LAFAYETTE CHILI (Circa Detroit - 1950's)

- 2-lbs ground beef
- 4 TB oil
- 2 envelopes onion soup mix
- 2 cups hot black coffee or Sanka
- 6-oz can tomato paste
- 2 TB chili powder
- 1 TB cumin powder
- ½-tsp garlic powder
- 1 tsp vinegar

Brown the beef in the oil, crumbling with fork till pink color disappears. Stir in onion soup mix & coffee, medium heat. Remove 1 cup of meat mixture to blender. Puree high speed till mixture resembles cement mortar. Return to remaining meat mixture & add remaining ingredients. Heat gently 1 hour. Serve in hot dog buns, hamburger buns or in in bowls. Serves 6

SLOPPY JOES — American Style

- 2-lbs ground round
- 4 TB oil
- 10-oz can tomato soup
- 14-oz can stewed tomatoes
- 2 envelopes onion soup mix
- ½-cup sweet pickle relish
- ½-cup ketchup
- 12-oz can V-8 Juice
- ¼-cup Grapenuts cereal
- 2 ribs celery minced fine

In large skilled brown beef in oil, crumbling with fork on med-high till pink color disappears. Stir in each remaining ingredient. Stir occasionally, cooking 1 hour on low heat. Spoon the mixture into split hamburger buns. Serves 6 satisfactorily—and freezes well in small portions to thaw & rewarm in 4 months.

BLENDER MINCED CELERY

For soups and sauces — quick and easily——Fill blender container half full cold water. Cut celery ribs into 2 or 3" lengths & drop into blender till water comes to within 1" of top. Cap tightly & blend high speed, on-off, 5 or 6 seconds—or till celery is size of confetti. Dump into fine mesh sieve or strainer & drain off water, reserving it if you wish to use in soups later. Use minced celery as individual recipes direct.

TOMATO SAUCE From Tomato Juice In A Pinch!

Break up 6 Ritz Crackers & drop into blender with ½-tsp season salt. Blend high speed till powdered. Heat 12-oz tomato juice—but don't boil—stirring in blender mixture, just till thickened & smooth. Remove at once from heat. Season to taste with salt & pepper. Makes 1/3 cup sauce. Use promptly.

TOTEM POLE POW WOW (Royal Oak, Mich - 1952)

At 1-inch intervals, make slits along one side of hot dog, only halfway through and grill so that hot dog curls into a circle, without falling apart. Place on large bun & spoon piping hot chili con carne into center topped with plenty of chopped fresh onions!!!

Best Sloppy Joe You'll Be Proud

BACON WRAPPED FRANKS IN BBQ SAUCE

Here is a super appetite appeaser and teaser to serve in your slow cooker to company on any occasion! Let the guests serve themselves. This recipe came from my sister, Hazel Allen, in Torrance, Calif., and even the most professional catering services could not do as well for an appetizer that will prompt everyone to ask for the recipe!

- 1-lb sliced bacon — each slice cut in half
- 1-lb Ball Park hot dogs - each hot dog in 3 equal pieces
- a box of round wooden toothpicks

- 3 cups ketchup
- 3 cups granulated sugar

Wrap one piece of the bacon around 1 piece of hot dog & secure with toothpick, placing these in a single layer in a large, shallow roasting pan. Bake them uncovered at 400F for 15 minutes or till bacon appears transparent and limp, and drippings cover the bottom of the pan. Remove the hot dog pieces to a slow cooker container, by lifting them out of the drippings using a pair of pliers, gripping the toothpick when transfering them. Don't fret about the toothpicks cooking right along with the food, as it will be perfectly all right. Discard the bacon drippings in that roasting pan. Combine the ketchup and sugar and pour over hot dog pieces. Cover slow cooker with tight fitting lid. Cook 1 hour on high and 7 to 8 hours on low, serving these right from the slow cooker, or transfer hot dog pieces and a little of the sauce to an electric skillet and keep on warm setting while serving them. Serves 6 beautifully!

HOT DOG! APPETIZER — Make-Ahead The Easy Way!

SNEAKY PETE'S is the brand name of a very special sauce, that isn't always available where I shop, so I learned how to make a close-kissin' cousin of this unique spicy sauce and I am perfectly willing to share the secret with all of you!

PESKY PETE'S PRACTICALLY PERFECT SAUCE

6-oz can tomato paste
4 tomato paste cans of water
½-cup ketchup
1 TB Worcestershire
2 TB Heinz 57 Sauce
1 TB chili powder
1½-tsp cumin powder
½-tsp garlic salt
¼-cup white vinegar
2 TB cornstarch

Add a pinch of Cajun

Cajun Seasoning: Combine ½ teaspoon *garlic salt*, ½ teaspoon ground *white pepper*, ½ teaspoon ground *red pepper*, ½ teaspoon ground *black pepper*, and ¼ teaspoon *dry mustard*.

Put all ingredients, as listed, into blender. Blend high speed, ½-a-minute or till smooth. Pour into 2½-qt saucepan & cook, stirring constantly, medium heat, till thickened & smooth, & comes to the 1st bubble of a boil! Remove from heat at once. Cool & funnel into bottle with tight-fitting cap. Keep refrigerated to use in 6 weeks. Freeze to thaw & use in 1 year. Makes about 5 cups of sauce.

ORIGINAL CHASE SONS CHILI

2½-lbs ground beef
1-lb ground pork
¼-cup oil
2 cups chopped onion
1 green pepper chopped
1½-tsp black pepper
1 tsp garlic powder
1-qt V-8 Juice
3 cans (14-oz each) stewed tomato
1-lb bag dry uncooked pinto beans
½-cup fresh chopped parsley
2 TB chili powder
2 tsp cumin powder
1 tsp MSG (optional)

In large skillet, brown the beef & pork in the oil, crumbling with fork on medium high heat, till pink color disappears. Stir in onion & green pepper, cooking till onion is tender. Transfer to Slow Cooker, adding each remaining ingredient, as listed. Do NOT presoak beans. Turn Slow Cooker to HIGH and cook covered for 4 hours. Then on LOW to cook for 12 to 15 hours. Serves 6 to 8 adequately. Freezes well in small portions to thaw & rewarm in 4 months.

most challenging
CHILI Inspired By Big Boy

With the help of oldest son, Bill, I worked & reworked this Make Alike to perfection!

In about 1 TB oil brown 1-lb ground round, crumbling with fork, in deep sided skillet or Dutch Oven. Turn to low while you open 2 cans (15-oz ea) light red kidney beans. Remove ½-cup of one can & set aside. Put remaining beans undrained into blender & blend high speed till finely pureed (1 min) & stir into browned beef, adding the beans you set aside. Then add 2½-TB chili powder, 1 TB paprika, 1 tsp cumin, ½-tsp salt, pepper to taste. Serve piping hot. Serves 6 sensibly.

This is a dish I concocted –from description – while visiting my sister, Hazel and our brother-in-law, Chris Allen, in Torrance, California, last May. Hazel wanted to have "chili" at the backyard barbecue, to spoon over the hamburgers and at first, I was thinking of chili the way we have it back here in Michigan. But what she meant was more like the Coney Sauce, that we enjoy here. So using what ingredients Hazel had on hand, I stirred together something that I spend all evening writing out the recipe for, so that everyone who tasted it, could have a copy. I didn't think it was going to be that great, really, but the family and our friends thought it was super!

California CHILI

2-lbs lean ground beef
2 TB oil
2 envelopes (1.5-oz ea) onion soup mix
32-oz jar Prego Spaghetti Sauce
2 cans (1-lb each) sliced style stewed tomatoes
1-TB chili powder
1½-tsp cumin powder
½-cup Port or Rose' wine (or cranberry juice instead)

In roomy skillet, brown beef in oil, crumbling till all pink color disappears, using med-high heat. Remove from heat. Transfer to a 4-quart cooking saucepan or kettle and add everything else. Let it cook without ever boiling, mind you, for 2 hours, uncovered. Stir it every so often. You can adjust the seasonings by adding more chili powder and cumin about 15 minutes before you plan to serve it. Serves 10 to 12 nicely. You can cut the recipe in half, or refrigerate leftovers covered tightly, to reheat within a week. Freeze any leftovers to thaw and rewarm within 3 months.

CHILI CON CARNE — Chili with beans, can be made by preparing the California Chili, exactly as directed above, and then stir into the finished mixture, 1 hour before serving, 4 cans (1-lb each) undrained red kidney beans. Continue as recipe otherwise directs.

SPAGHETTI SAUCE FROM CALIFORNIA CHILI

Prepare the California Chili, just as above recipe directs, but to serve it over cooked, drained, thin spaghetti, you should also stir into the sauce, as the last ingredients, 2/3 cup bottled Italian Salad Dressing, 3 TB sugar, ¼-cup Coca-Cola or black coffee. Continue as recipe above otherwise directs. Sufficient to serve, spooned over 2-lbs cooked, drained, thin spaghetti or other shaped pasta. Refrigerate or freeze leftover sauce in accordance with California Chili recipe directions.

CHILI

BARBECUE SAUCE DRY MIX

4 TB brown sugar, packed
1 tsp black pepper
2 tsp chili powder
1 tsp hickory flavored salt
1 tsp garlic powder

Stir all ingredients well. Multiply recipe according to needs. Makes 1/3 cup of sauce mix.

TO USE BBQ SAUCE MIX: Combine all of above recipe (1/3 cup) with a 14-oz bottle ketchup, 1 TB light vinegar, stirring well. Cover and chill 1 hour before using. Makes about a pint.

THE RESTAURANT
Gloria Pitzer's Copycat Cookbook

FRANKENMUTH CHICKEN NOODLE SOUP (From Scratch)

- 5-lbs cut-up chicken fryer parts
- 1 large white onion quartered
- 4 peppercorns or ½-tsp pepper
- 3 quarts water
- 1 dry bay leaf
- Salt to taste
- 3 carrots cut-up fine
- 1 small bunch celery with leaves - diced

(See Note below for using additional flavoring.)

Put everything into an accomodating kettle. Bring to boil. Boil 1 minute & reduce to gentle simmer. Cover kettle with lid. Simmer 2 hours. Stir it occasionally. With slotted spoon, remove chicken & vegetables from the broth. Dice the white meat & set aside. Discard skin & bones. Dice Dice some of the carrots to your liking & set aside. Discard the rest. Put broth through coffee-filter-lined sieve, catching cleared broth in another kettle the same size. Chill till all fat comes to top & is solid & can be removed. Return to heat. Add chicken & carrots. Bring to boil. PREPARE NOODLES—Mound 1 cup flour on a board. Make well in center. Add 1 egg to that well, with ¼-tsp salt & 1 TB cold water. Gradually work into a smooth dough. Knead till smooth, adding enough more flour to keep from being sticky. Wrap dough in waxed paper. Let stand 1 hour at room tem. On floured surface roll dough paper thin. Roll up jelly roll style & slice into thin strips, unwrapping into long noodles. Snip into shorter lengths. Drop into simmering soup. Allow 18 to 22 minutes simmering approximately—or till noodles are tender to the bite (al dente'). Serve soup piping hot. Refrigerate leftover soup, tightly covered, to rewarm in 4 or 5 days. Freeze to thaw & reheat in 4 months. Makes 12 servings. NOTE: For additional flavoring in the broth, add 4 or 5 packets of Herb Ox Chicken Broth Powder — or 2 TB low-salt chicken bouillon powder. For richer flavor, add 3 packets Sweet & Low or 2 tsp sugar. Season Salt or Mrs. Dash may also be added to taste.

SLOW COOKER CHILI CON CARNE

Denny's chili is thick and rich and spicy, laced with cheese— a meal in itself. Big Boy's chili is also very Mexican, compared to the East Coast style of Chili Con Carne (with beans) but of all the recipes —from every restaurant that has ever impressed me with their chili offering, here is an inspired version that we make in the Slow Cooker, taking anywhere from 12 to 24 hours, as you wish, letting it cook on LOW overnight as well.

Measure the capacity of your Slow Cooker. This recipe will accomodate a 14-cup cooker.

- 2-lbs ground round
- 2 TB oil

- 2 cans (14-oz each) sliced style stewed tomatoes
- 10-oz can beef gravy
- 2 envelopes onion soup mix
- 3 cans (1-lb each) red beans or kidney beans, undrained
- 2 TB chili powder
- 1 TB ground cumin

- 2-lb jar Prego Spaghetti Sauce Flavored With Meat
- 1 cup coffee or Sanka—prepared, hot or cold

In medium skillet, brown the ground round in the oil, crumbly with fork till all pink color disappears. Pour into Slow Cooker & turn heat to high, adding each remaining ingredient as listed. Stir to combine thoroughly. Cook, covered on HIGH 2 hours. Turn to LOW & allow to cook anywhere from 12 to 24 hours, as you wish. Freeze in small portions to thaw & gently heat within 90 days. Makes 10 healthy-sized servings!

TERRIFIC

BARBECUED BEEF

Prepare the Fall Apart Beef Roast and refrigerate it overnight, before preparing the Barbecued Beef from part of it. The refrigeration will help to tenderize the beef.

Cut lean pieces of the chilled roast into 1 to 1½-inch chunks and then shred these pieces into strands of beef, using 2 forks to separate the grain this way. When you have 4 cups of shredded beef, transfer to a large skillet.

OUR WAY

Add 2 cups water & bring to boil, simmering gently uncovered, 10 minutes, stirring frequently. Turn heat to low and stir in 1 cup each:
- bottled apple butter
- Catalina Dressing
- Ketchup

Stir to combine ingredients. Cover with a lid and allow to cook gently on lowest heat about an hour. Stir once in a-while. Serve the beef mixture spooned into split hamburger or onion rolls. Serves 4 to 6.

EXTRA SPICY BBQ BEEF ...
When you stir in the 3 sauce ingredients, also add ¼-cup of Heinz 57 Sauce, 1 TB Worcestershire, 1 TB A-1 Sauce, 2 TB brown sugar. Heat gently as directed in above recipe.

FALL APART BEEF ROAST
(Old-Fashioned Pot Roast)

FOR A ROAST that practically falls apart at the touch of the fork, try this recipe-technique. The more lean the meat, of course, the more tender, but you don't have to stick with the traditional cuts of English, Round Bone or Chuck Roasts. You might have less waste and shrinkage if you were to select a medium priced cut of beef, such as Heel of Boneless Round, or Sirloin. Peeled, cut up fresh carrots and peeled quartered, large baking potatoes can be arranged around the meat for the last 1½-hours of the roasting time.

- 3-to-5-lb beef roast
- ¼-cup oil
- 2 tsp season salt (or to taste)

Place the roast, best-side-up in an accomdating roasting pan that has a tight fitting lid. Cover the top of the beef in the oil and dust it with the season salt. Place it about 4" from broiler heat, to sear the top side only, until browned and crispy looking. Lower the roasting pan to center rack. Put the lid on the pan. Turn off broiler heat and turn on oven heat to 375F—for 20 minutes. Then reduce heat to 300F—allowing 35 minutes per pound. You do not have to turn the roast during baking time. But during last hour of baking, baste it often in the pan juices. If the beef is lacking in juice add a 14-oz can of clear beef broth —or chicken broth, to be certain there is sufficient liquid in the pan. The liquid should fill the pan half-full around the roast. You may also sprinkle on 1 envelope of onion soup mix, if you wish, or cut up 2 or 3 white crisp onions, each about the size of an orange and place around the roast about half-way through the baking time.

Serves 4 to 6 with leftovers that will keep if refrigerated & tightly covered, up to a week—OR freeze the leftovers to be used within 3 months.

SHORTCUTS WITH STYLE

BARBECUED BEEF SAUCE
Another good sauce recipe to use instead of the basic 3 ingredients listed above, is to add 1 pint of bottled barbecue sauce (like Open Pit) plus 8-oz can jellied cranberry sauce, well-mashed with fork, plus ¼-cup packed light brown sugar, & 2 TB vinegar. Heat gently as otherwise directed in recipe given above.

Freeze sauce in small portions to thaw & rewarm within 4 months.

Frankenmuth Bavarian Family Restaurant — What better, easier way — BARBECUE — The Recipe Detective

BEEF

ROAST BEEF (Prime Rib)

Try the technique with a no-rib roast, such as a Sirloin Tip. When you find joy in n-o-t cooking anymore than you have to, this roast practically makes itself and requires only a minimum of attention and details.

7 to 8-lb Sirloin Tip Roast
2 cloves garlic
½-cup oil
½-tsp season salt

Pierce roast with 2-tined carving set fork in 20 or 30 places on all sides. Place cloves of garlic, sliced into halves, in oil, in 12" skillet. Heat oil to almost smoking, remove garlic as soon as it "sizzles"! Heat intensifies the odor and flavor of garlic, so do not let it remain in the hot oil too long. It might just drive you right out of the kitchen, depending on the strength of the cloves you are using. Aged, dry garlic bulbs have more strength than the freshly picked garlic.

Now brown all sides of roast in hot oil mixture until each side is crispy and place roast, best-side-up on a rack in shallow roasting pan. Bake in preheated 300F—oven, uncovered, 25 minutes per pound, without turning the roast at all during baking—for rare. 30 mins per-lb for med-rare; 35 mins per-lb for med-well and 40-mins per-lb for well. And with that you're on your own—or heading for pot roast possibilities with a well done Sirloin Tip!!! Allow ½-lb per serving. Let roast stand 20 minutes in the roasting pan, before attempting to slice it.

LEFTOVERS may be refrigerated to be used within a week—OR freeze them to be used within 3 months.

beef in a whole new way...

IF ROAST IS TOO RARE

If you cut into the roast and find center is more rare than you like, place slices on cookie sheet about 2" from boiler heat for a minute or two or to desired doneness and then serve promptly. The beef should be more rare when you slice it than you want it to be when you eat it, for as the beef sits, sliced, on a serving platter, it re-absorbs some of its own juices and you'll notice that 10 minutes after slicing it, it appears to be less red, than when first sliced. It continues to cook in its own heat during this time.

EASY SHORTCUTS WITH STYLE

BLENDER GRAVY
GROOVY GRAVY

This is a fast blender gravy, although you can whip it up with an electric mixer on high speed, but you will then have to pour it through a strainer to be certain all particles are removed that did not dissolve while beating it.

BEEF GRAVY

2 cans (14-oz ea) clear beef broth
1½-tsp Kitchen Bouquet liquid
1 TB beef bouillon powder
¾-cup biscuit mix
2 tsp onion powder

Blend all ingredients till smooth, using high speed of blender about 1 minute. Pour mixture into 2-qt saucepan, stirring it constantly over medium high till it thickens and is smooth (about 6 to 8 minutes.) Makes about 5 cups of gravy. In tightly covered container it can be refrigerated to be used within 1 week. Freeze to use within 3 months.

THE BEST

When you cook without complications, you compile in your file, those recipes that don't have a long list of ingredients and those that you can put-together in a pinch and know they'll do you proud! Some of my favorites for this file of reliables are not maindish ideas that stand well by themselves, alone, on my table, but those that make a dish that's simple, seem more than ample.

Western Barbecue

1 cup Ketchup
1 cup Catalina Salad Dressing
1 cup bottled apple butter
½-cup A-1 Steak Sauce
½-cup Coca-Cola
2 TB Worcestershire Sauce

Mix it all together thoroughly. Store it in a quart jar with a tight fitting lid and keep it refrigerated to use within a month. Makes a quart.

PORK CHOP BBQ — Successful

TO USE THE BBQ SAUCE, when you bake plain pork chops in a shallow roasting pan, having chops in a single layer, wipe the surface of each chop with a tablespoon or two of the sauce. Bake uncovered at 375F—about 45 minutes and add more sauce to the chops as you wish, applying it about every 10 or 15 minutes during baking. Do not turn the chops during baking. When you serve the pork chops, surround them on a lovely platter, with whole boiled new potatoes, in or out of their jackets. Or boil some broad egg noodles and drain them well and make a snowbank-type arrangement of the noodles around the pork chops, overlapping them down the center of a big oval serving platter. Sprinkle the noodles with some toasted sesame seeds, a little dry minced parsley, rubbed to a fine dust between your fingers, or some flecks of season salt and a drizzling of butter. Allow 1 chop per serving, if they are cut pretty thick, but allow 2 if they are thin chops and then, of course, reduce baking time, accordingly.

SLOPPY JOE BBQ — Heavy Duty

A bit more mild than the Coney Sauce, you can brown 2-pounds of ground round or ground chuck in a few tablespoons of oil in a roomy skillet, mashing it with a fork, till the pink color disappears. Use medium high heat for this and then turn to lowest possible heat and stir in a 10-oz can tomato soup and 1 cup of the BBQ Sauce, and let it fend for itself, covered with a nice-fitting lid, cooking slowly on low for about an hour before you spoon it into split hamburger buns. Serve something like this sandwich with coleslaw or our potato salad, or a bowl of piping hot gussied-up canned soup.

CHICKEN IN BBQ SAUCE

Prepare the baked chicken breasts as I describe somewhere in this book, and then 15 minutes before the baking time is scheduled to expire, dab a tablespoon of the BBQ Sauce over each piece of the chicken. You don't want to add it too soon or it may scorch and have a bitter taste. All you want to do with it is get it warmed when you baste the food in it. The top of the stove approach with the Sloppy Joe recipe, however, gives you the tomato soup with which to dilute the sauce, and the lowest possible heat for tenderizing the ground beef, which is a bit different than the oven-baked treatment.

BEST-EVER BARBECUES

Gloria Pitzer's Copycat Cookbook — Pages 13 & 14

RIBS IN BBQ SAUCE

4 to 5-lb slab of ribs
1 cup ketchup
1 cup bottled applebutter
1 cup Catalina Salad Dressing
2 tsp hickory flavored salt
2 TB dark molasses
10-oz can Franco American Beef Gravy

1 envelope onion soup mix
6-oz can V-8 juice
½-tsp Worcestershire
½-tsp Heinz 57 Sauce
½-tsp A-1 Steak Sauce

Cut the rib slab into 3 or 4 rib portions so that it will be more easily handled. Place in ungreased shallow roasting pan, large enough to accomodate the ribs in a single layer. Combine remaining ingredients. Bake the ribs uncovered, at 350F—basted generously in the sauce—every 15 minutes for almost 2 hours—or till tender, bubbly and well browned. Allow 1-lb per serving.

Barbecue Sauce In minutes.

TENNESSEE BROWN BARBECUE SAUCE

A favorite of Down Home Restaurants, poured over sandwiches and used to baste spare ribs, chicken and steaks.

Mix together 10-oz can Franco American Beef Gravy with 2½-cups Basic BBQ Sauce and 1½-tsp hickory flavored salt (NOT liquid) and 1 TB dark molasses. Makes almost a quart. Keep it refrigerated. Use within 6 weeks.

Good. Harmony

BASIC BBQ SAUCE — Barbecue

1 cup bottled applebutter
1 cup bottled Catalina Salad Dressing
1 cup ketchup (Heinz preferred)

Stir these ingredients together well. Keep tightly covered and refrigerated to be used within 6 weeks. Makes 3 cups sauce.

SAURKRAUT (With or Without Spareribs)

Hamtramck Style — like Under The Eagle serves!

2 cans (28-oz ea) saurkraut   4 TB packed brown sugar
2 cans (14-oz ea) beef broth   1 TB dry minced onion
1 peeled raw medium potato   1 TB caraway seed (optional)
1 peeled raw medium apple   4-lbs spare ribs (approx)

Drain & rinse kraut in cold water, squeezing out all liquid. Combine with broth in large greased baking dish. Grate potato & apple on large hole of vegetable grater & add to kraut with brown sugar, onion & the caraway seed. Arrange ribs over top of kraut (meat side of ribs up & cut into 2 or 3 bone sections). Dust evenly in paprika if you wish & bake uncovered 350F—about 2 hours or till ribs are tender & brown. Serves 4 to 6. Kraut may be prepared without ribs or with 3 to 4-lbs kielbasa in 2" lengths, instead of ribs.

Snack! Quick

SHRIMP ON A BRICK

Disappears fast! Great for Sunday night supper appetizer.

8-oz pkg cream cheese
10-oz bottle Heinz cocktail sauce
10-oz bottle Heinz chili sauce
1½-to-2-lbs frozen, cooked shrimp

Place cream cheese unwrapped, but in one piece in center of serving plate. Mix 2 sauces together. Thaw & DRAIN WELL the shrimp & add to sauce. Pour over cream cheese. Surround with assorted crackers & add 2 or 3 butter knives to the cheese to let everyone help themselves, spreading it onto the crackers. Serves 6 senislby or 2 foolishly. Keep refrigerated. Use in a few days.

SHORT RIBS IN BBQ SAUCE

6 to 8-lbs beef short ribs
1 cup Catalina Salad Dressing
1 cup Ketchup
1 cup bottled apple butter
12-oz can 7-UP

Easy

Simmer the short ribs in enough water to keep them submerged, in a covered kettle on top of the stove—about 15 mins. Drain water & keep it refrigerated in covered container to use later in which to boil cabbage or potatoes to accompany the short ribs. Arrange drained pieces of the ribs in an accomdating roasting pan with a lid. Combine remaining ingredients & pour over ribs, repeating the sauce mixture as necessary to adequately cover the ribs. Bake covered at 325F—5 hours. Baste every so often in the pan sauces & drippings. Refrigerate 24 hours & return to bake at 350F—1½-hrs before serving. Serves 10 to 12.

BARBECUE SAUCE FOR RIBS

This sauce can be made in smaller quantities for immediate use, but the savings is in making it for the freezer. It reminds me a good bit of the famous Cattleman's Brand, but is purely the creation of Chef Bill Payne.

In an accomodating kettle combine the following ingredients:

46-oz can tomato juice   4-oz prepared mustard
14-oz bottle ketchup   4 TB season salt
5-oz A1 Sauce   1 onion the size of an egg—chopped
5-oz Heinz 57 Sauce   6 whole cloves garlic, peeled
5-oz Worcestershire Sauce   1 cup packed brown sugar
4-oz white vinegar   4 TB lemon juice
21-oz water   3 dry bay leaves

Bring mixture to a full boil, stirring to combine mixture. Turn heat to low and allow to simmer about 5 minutes, stirring frequently so it won't scorch. Cool to lukewarm. Add Tabasco Sauce to taste if you wish. Divide mixture into family sized containers to freeze to be used within 1 year. Makes about 3 quarts.

Top Secret Recipes REMEMBER

PANTRY VEGETABLE CASSEROLE
(Smith's Pantry-Pt.Huron, Mich)

What made this unique from other restaurant dishes that might be similar, is the appealing freshness & crisp texture of the vegetables. Pantry dishes were always excellent. To serve 6 sufficiently, slice 1 long thin zucchini, unpeeled, paper thin & mix lightly with 2 cans (14-oz ea) sliced style stewed tomatoes, 10-oz pkg frozen, thawed broccoli spears, cutting each spear into 4 pieces, plus 4 ribs celery, sliced paper thin. Then cut a 10-oz box frozen cauliflower into small bits, about the size of thimbles. Add to the zucchini mixture. Season lavishly with salt & pepper or to taste. Add a pinch of Rosemary leaves, 1 clove garlic sliced thin. Cover & bake in greased casserole, 375F-about 45 mins & stir it once in awhile during baking. Divide mixture then equally between 6 greased oven-proof soup bowls. Sprinkle top of each in a little shredded Mozzarella. Place bowls about 6" from broiler heat just to melt the cheese. Serve promptly. Refrigerate leftovers to use in a few days. Do not freeze.

CHICKEN SALAD
Like J.L. Hudson's Detroit 1950's

Combine 1-lb can drained Mandarin orange sections & 1-lb can drained pineapple chunks, 4 cups cut-up, cooked, white chicken meat & ½-cup sliced almonds. Make a dressing of 1 cup sour cream, 1 cup mayonnaise, ½-cup sweet orange marmalade, 1/8-tsp poultry seasoning. Mix well & pour over chicken mixture, coating well. Cover & refrigerate 24 hrs before serving. Serves 8. 2 cups fresh green grapes can be added to this as was done when grapes were in season. Slicing grapes in half will emit more of the juice.

MAID RITE is the name of a hamburger chain that served a loose hamburger, slightly seasoned, but not like the traditional Coney Sauce that we are most often used to. A letter from one of our radio family, Mrs. Nadermann in Dubuque, Iowa, told us her father had a store just around the corner from a Maid-Rite in Dubuque and they frequented the hamburger place often. It was not in the least like a Sloppy Joe mixture. According to Mrs. Nadermann you browned 1½ to 2-lbs ground beef in a roomy skillet, with perhaps 2 TB of oil, crumbling the beef with the back of a fork, over moderate heat, until all of the pink color disappears. Add 1 diced onion (about the size of an egg) and a 14-oz can of clear chicken broth. Simmer the mixture uncovered, on very low heat, until most of the broth has been absorbed by the beef & onions. Ladle a good measure of this mixture onto a hamburger bun and top it off with prepared yellow mustard and dill pickle chips. Mrs. Nadermann tells us you can add ketchup and fresh diced onions also, if you wish. The secret, she said, however, is in using the chicken broth, and I agree. The formula is right "on target"!

GREENFIELD'S HOT CHICKEN SALAD
(Detroit Circa: 1950's)

- 10-oz can Cream Chicken Soup
- ½-soup can mayonnaise
- 1½-cups diced cooked chicken (or 6-oz can boneless chicken)
- 2 ribs celery diced fine
- 2 TB dry minced onions
- ½-cup "hammered" Smoke House Almonds (BBQ flavored)
- 6 strips bacon fried crispy & crumbled—OR 2½-oz can Broadcast brand real crumbled bacon —not artificial bits

Heat soup and mayonnaise over hot water in top of double boiler, combining thoroughly with rubber bowl scraper till smooth. (Do not use direct heat when dish contains mayonnaise). Stir in remaining ingredients. Keep it piping hot over the simmering water, about 30 minutes before serving. Serve it spooned into lettuce leaf lined plates, with slices of canned jellied cranberry sauce on the side and bottled, drained, spiced apples slices as garnish. Crumble hard cooked egg yolk over top and dust lightly in paprika and parsley flakes. Serves 4.

MARINATED CHICKEN - How To Prepare...

Melt ¼-lb margarine (not butter for it burns) in a 12" skillet along with ¼-cup oil. Coat the moist chicken pieces, just removed from the marinade, into a shallow dish of Bisquick. Coat lightly but evenly. Brown pieces over medium heat till browned on all sides. Do not use high heat or it will strengthen garlic flavor and aroma too much. See my notes on garlic in beginning of this book. Transfer browned pieces to greased baking pan. Cover loosely in foil. Keep warm at 325F— till all pieces have been browned and then keep in warm oven no longer than 30 mins before serving. Refrigerate leftovers, well-covered, to rewarm within 3 or 4 days. Serves 4 to 6.

BARBECUED CHICKEN can be prepared with the marinated, skinless, boneless chicken breasts, by removing them from marinade & placing in single layer in greased 9" square baking dish. Make a sauce by combining 1 cup each bottled Heinz Chili Sauce, bottled seafood cocktail sauce, ketchup & strawberry jam. Spoon over chicken. Seal dish in foil & bake at 325F—for 1½-hours. Remove foil. Bake uncovered about 10 mins, to let sauce bubble. Serves 4 to 6.

POACHING CHICKEN FOR CHICKEN SALAD

Do not marinate the chicken pieces, but place 6 boneless, skinless chicken breasts in a 12" skillet and pour a 14-oz can clear chicken broth over them. Cover the skillet. Simmer 10 minutes. Turn pieces & cover & simmer another 10 minutes. Remove from heat. Cool to lukewarm. Refrigerate chicken in the simmering liquids in covered container. Chicken should be thoroughly chilled before preparing for salad (about 2 or 3 hours of refrigeration).

CHICKEN IMPROVEMENT

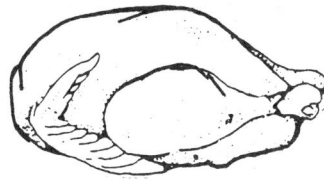

PUT AWAY CHICKEN — EASIEST CHICKEN

1½-to-2-lbs chicken breasts (about 4 breast halves)

Enough water to cover 1" above pieces in an accomodating kettle (About 10 cups)

2 tsp season salt (or to taste)
½-tsp pepper
1 onion the size of an egg—peeled & cut in half

Combine it all nicely over high heat in the accomodating kettle and bring it to a boil. At once turn heat low enough to produce a very gentle simmer. Cover the kettle with a tight fitting lid and allow it to simmer gently about 40 minutes or till chicken is tender. Remove chicken pieces from the broth and refrigerate these in doubled plastic bag, tightly sealed, to be used within 4 days in another recipe.

GRAVY IN A PINCH

Couldn't ask for a better can-opener gourmet gravy than opening a 10-oz can Franco American Beef Gravy and combining it in a 1½-qt saucepan with 10-oz can Franco American Chicken Gravy, 10-oz can cream of celery soup, 2 tsp bottled Kitchen Bouquet, 1 tsp onion salt—or to taste. Add 2 TB butter or margrine and heat gently, stirring constantly. Makes about 6 servings. Leftover gravy will keep, if refrigerated, up to 2 weeks.

QUICHE

BROCCOLI QUICHE
Inspired By Bill Knapp's

A deep dish Pet Ritz 9" pie shell thawed but unbaked
1 TB coffee cream

¼-cup coffee cream (½ & ½ will do)
4 large eggs (5 medium-sized eggs)
4-oz pkg shredded Cheddar cheese
10-oz pkg frozen chopped broccoli partially thawed & undrained
¼-tsp season salt (or Mrs. Dash)
black pepper to taste

Preheat oven to 375F—. Prick the unbaked pie shell with a fork in 20 or 30 places. Wipe surface lightly but evenly with the 1 TB coffee cream & pour out excess. Gently blot up any visible excess cream from the surface of pie shell with paper towel. Place on cookie sheet and bake 5 minutes exactly at 375F.

While pie shell is baking, put cream & eggs into blender, blending high speed 1 minute. Turn off motor & add cheese. Blend ½-minute on high speed. Add HALF of the package of chopped broccoli, blending ½-minute longer. Add season salt & pepper & blend ½-minute more. Remove blender from motor area & use knife to stir in remaining chopped broccoli. Set aside while you remove the partially baked pie shell from oven at the end of the 5-minute baking time. The crust will be puffed and will raise a few inches from the pan. Gently pierce the puffed area with tip of sharp knife in 4 or 5 places till crust settles back into place again. Press it gently into place with fingers & pour in the blender mixture. Bake the filled pie shell on the cookie sheet, at 375F—for 45 minutes or till knife inserted in center comes out clean and top is set and golden brown. Cool in the pie on the cookie sheet on wire rack for 10 minutes before cutting to serve 6.

MARINADE FOR CHICKEN

Chef Dan Gallagher's Chicken Marinade

Whenever I'm baffled by a recipe imitation, I try to consult with our friend, the chef at the Village Inn, right here in St. Clair. And while I am busy working with a dozen possible ingredients, Chef Dan Gallagher can come up with the result I'm looking for, but using only a few ingredients. Dan says that marinating chicken in fruit juices can be tricky since fruit juice "burns"—but his simple combination proved to be exactly what we wanted in order to imitate the popular El Pollo chains that are quickly moving from the West Coast to the East with as much fanfare as the recent Cajun units.

½-cup orange juice
1 TB honey
1/8 tsp paprika
pinch of salt

what a good idea!

(optional — the juice of ½-a-lemon or juice of 1 whole lime)

Combine ingredients, repeating the recipe as needed to coat chicken pieces, refrigerating these in the marinade in covered non-metal container with tight-fitting lid—up to 24 hours before preparing. 8 hours for small servings of 4 to 6 pieces, but as long as 24 hours for 2 cut-up chicken fryers—about 15 pieces.

BROIL Chicken

Remove chicken pieces from marinade. Char-broil or flame broil, or in electric oven, placed skin-side up, 6" from broiler heat for 6 to 8 minutes. Cover chicken loosely in foil & bake about 30 minutes—or till tender—at 375F—testing thickest part of meat with knife to be certain it is done.

BARBECUED CHICKEN — Spicy

3-lb cut-up chicken fryer or favorite chicken parts
½-cup Heinz 57 Sauce
¼-cup honey
8-oz bottle Catalina Dressing

Arrange chicken pieces skin-side-up in Pam-sprayed shallow roasting pan. Combine last 3 ingredients, stirring well. Brush mixture evenly over skin of chicken pieces. Bake uncovered, without turning pieces, at 375F—1 hour & 15 minutes or till golden brown and crispy. Baste chicken in additional sauce mixture about every 10 minutes during baking. Serves 4.

TESTED RECIPES
updated best-kept secrets

WING DINGS/Buffalo Style
Many food artists fail to realize the big difference between authentic Buffalo (NY) wings and just spicy coated fried chicken wings, brand-named "Wing Dings". Wing Dings are coated like our traditional recipe for fried chicken, but Buffalo Wings are never breaded. At the time of this writing Ponderosa has the best to offer on their buffet.

BUFFALO WINGS New York Style
Cut off & discard boney tip of a dozen chicken wings. Split wings at the joint. Fry in 385F- hot oil few mins till golden brown. Remove from oil. Drain on paper towel. In saucepan on medium heat, warm small bottle Durkee brand RED HOT SAUCE & 1/4-lb butter till melted. Coat wings in sauce. Arrange in single layer in shallow baking pan. Bake slowly, uncovered, 250F to 275F 30 to 40 mins till sauce is completely baked into wings. Serve promptly with your favorite dipping sauce or blue cheese dressing. For 4.

HONEY BAKED CHICKEN
In Pam-sprayed oblong baking pan arrange 3-1b cut-up chicken fryer, skin side up, single layer. Wipe each piece in a little oil. Dust in season salt. Bake uncovered 375F- about 45 mins. Make a sauce by combining 1/2-cup ketchup, 1/4-cup A-1 Steak Sauce, 1/4-cup honey. Spoon evenly on each piece & continue baking them 15 to 20 mins longer uncovered or till browned. Serve with additional heated sauce on the side. Another way to do honey baked chicken is to combine equal parts DIONAISSE & honey, coating each piece chicken, skin-side upafter the 1st 45 mins of baking as described above. Omit sauce altogether on this version & bake about 30 mins or till golden brown to your liking.

CHICKEN PATTY PARMESAN
If you have enjoyed a good Veal Parmesan dish, such as they serve at Big Boy Restaurants, then you might like to try the idea using the ready to brown, frozen chicken patties. They're nicely coated and Swanson puts out a very good frozen product, I feel. Prepare the patties as the box directs and arrange one patty on an oven-proof platter or stainless steel platter. Spread some gently heated Prego Spaghetti Sauce over each patty and then a slice of Mozzerella and just a little dab more of the sauce on top of the cheese — A dab, now, please. Place about 6-inches from the broiler heat till cheese is melted, taking perhaps, 4 or 5 minutes, if that long. Serve at once with a nice tossed salad and a smooth fruity dessert, rather than something heavy. OR you can serve a small portion of very thin spaghetti that you've cooked per box directions and drained well, along with more heated Prego sauce over that to accompany the chicken patty

COOKING LESSON — HOW TO COOK SPAGHETTI
While I mention thin spaghetti to you, let me elaborate on how you cook it. The box will give you specific instructions, but I usually put about 8 cups of water in my 2½-qt saucepan for every 8-oz box of THIN spaghetti. Add 1 tsp salt to that water and 2 TB oil, for the oil prevents the spaghetti from sticking together as it is cooking. Fan the spaghetti pieces when you place them in the water, being certain that it has come to a brisk boil, before adding the spaghetti. Gently push down on the tops of the strands of spaghetti, forcing them g-e-n-t-l-y into the boiling water, without breaking them. As the part of the strands soften that are in the water, the upper part can be pushed down to become submerged, as well. Set your timer for 8 minutes, letting the spaghetti boil gently uncovered. Then the only way to really test it for doneness is to taste a strand, biting into it. My Aunt Angela says that is called "Al Dente"—to the bite. The texture should be firm, but not hard and yet a bit chewy but not soft or mushy.

If you don't want your spaghetti swimming in liquids, which only make the sauce you will add to it, very runny, then dump the spaghetti into a large sieve (strainer) and do NOT rinse under tap water — ever — for you only wash away the important fiber and vitamins. You merely want to get rid of the starchy cooking water. So shake that spaghetti vigorously back and forth, from side to side, in the strainer and then dump it quickly into your serving bowl, or onto your platter — as you prefer. Spoon some of the sauce over the top of the spaghetti, to within 2" of the edge, allowing a nice eye appeal in the contrast of the red sauce and white pasta. Sprinkle some canned grated Parmesan over the center of the sauce or dump an 8-oz can of saucepan-warmed mushrooms into the center if you wish and MONJA! Eat! And enjoy!

Italian — QUICK BLENDER SPAGHETTI SAUCE
1-lb jar Prego Spaghetti Sauce
½-cup Concord Grape Wine
1 envelope (1.5-oz) onion soup mix
10-oz can tomato soup

Put all 4 ingredients through blender on high speed till smooth. Meanwhile brown a pound of ground beef in a bit of oil till pink color disappears, crumbling with fork. Add blender mixture. Heat gently. Sufficient to spoon over 1-lb cooked, drained pasta.

CHICKEN CHOW MEIN
Borrowing the sauce ingredient ratio from the Shrimp Ala King recipe, this is how I prepare this dish.

Put a 14½-oz can clear chicken broth into blender with 3 level TB cornstarch and 1/3 cup lightly brewed tea — preferably cooled down to lukewarm. Blend these ingredients on high about ½-a-minute or till smooth. Pour into a 1½-qt saucepan and cook over medium-high, stirring constantly till smooth. Let it boil only ½-a-minute and remove from heat at once. Stir in a 6½-oz can boned chicken in broth or about 1¼-cups well-diced, leftover, baked white chicken meat, minus bones and skin. Add a TB dry minced onion and a 4-oz can well drained mushrooms if you wish or small can drained sliced water chestnuts if you like those. Or use about 2/3 cup of cooked celery, prepared per that recipe in this book. Keep the mixture on lowest possible heat till time to serve, up to 1 hour and spoon it nicely over canned Chow Mein or Rice Noodles. Rice Noodles from LaChoy, look like Chow Mein noodles, if you have never tried them before. But they are thinner and a bit more crisp than the Chow Mein noodle and I like them tossed into salads, too. The Big Boy restaurants usually offer them on their salad bars. This recipe nicely accomodates 4 reasonable appetites.

LASAGNA WITHOUT COOKING THE NOODLES

This recipe I borrowed from good friend Irma Lumsden, whose mother is the author of the lovely book of devotional poems that I tell you about in this issue. I love the simplicity of this tasty dish and the fact that at our Good Sam Potluck at our Bay City ralley, this was one of two dishes out of the 50 on the table, to disappear before I had a chance to even taste but a spoonful of it. You'll love it!

3 TB oil
1-lb ground round
1 envelope onion soup mix
14½-oz can sliced style stewed tomatoes
27½-oz can Hunt's Spaghetti Sauce

8-oz box lasagna noodles - DO NOT COOK

1½-cup pkg shredded Monterey Jack cheese
2 cups pkg shredded Mozzarella & Provolone cheese

In large skillet heat oil & brown ground beef in this on medium high, crumbling with fork, till pink color disappears. Stir in soup mix, stewed tomatoes & canned (or homemade) spaghetti sauce. Heat thorough, about 5 minutes. Remove from heat. Spread about ½-cup of the sauce evenly over bottom of Pam-sprayed deep oven dish. (Mine measures about 9" in diameter & 3½" deep.) Then break up about a third of the noodles to fit over the sauce evenly. Then another portion of sauce and next sprinkle on about a third of the cheese, which I mixed together first in a medium bowl. Repeat the layers to fill the bowl in this manner: Sauce — broken noodles — Sauce — Cheese. With the last layer of the broken noodles, use both of your hands to press down on the mixture to make room for the last addition of sauce & cheese. Then bake uncovered at 350F—1 hour & 10 minutes. After 45 minutes, be sure to cover the baking dish with foil, greased on dull side in Pam & placed dull-side down over the Lasagna. Serves 4 to 6 adequately. Refrigerate the leftovers to rewarm within 3 or 4 days. Freeze to thaw & rewarm in 3 months.

PASTA

VEGETABLE LASAGNA 3rd Day/Make/Bake

The Vegetable Lasagna that a frozen food company has been known for inspired my 1st version of this. The Voyageur's version, however, inspired this updated version.

INGREDIENTS:
8-oz box UNCOOKED lasagna noodles
The Sauce (recipe follows)
Ricotta Mixture (recipe follows)
12-oz Mozzarella sliced or shredded
A little grated Parmesan
4½-oz jar sliced mushrooms, drained

THE SAUCE:
14-oz can stewed tomatoes
26-oz can Hunt's Spaghetti Sauce
4½-oz jar sliced mushrooms, drained
1/4-cup sliced green stuffed olives
1/4-cup sliced, pitted ripe olives
8-oz can (small size) sliced carrots, drained & cut-up

Combine all sauce ingredients as listed. Use per directions below.

RICOTTA MIXTURE:
15-oz carton ricotta cheese
1 egg

Beat together with mixer on med-speed till smooth. Set aside & use per recipe directions below.

THE ORDER IN WHICH YOU ASSEMBLE THIS IS CRITICAL!
Grease a 10x13x2" baking pan. Assemble as follows:

HALF OF SAUCE spread evenly over bottom
HALF of uncooked noodles in single layer over sauce
HALF of ricotta mixture evenly over noodles
HALF of Mozzarella over that
Then rest of noodles, RICOTTA MIXTURE, Mozzarella & the sauce LAST before sprinkling it with Parmesan and arranging the 2nd jar of sliced, drained mushrooms on top. Seal in foil. Refrigerate 2 to 3 days. Uncover & bake at 350F- about an hour, till golden & bubbly. Let stand 15 mins before cutting to serve. Refrigerate leftovers to use in a few days. Freeze in serving size portions to use in a few months. Makes 8 to 10 servings.

Out-of-the-Ordinary

ITALIAN Side Dishes Deception

CAVATINI
(A pasta dish inspired by Pizza Hut!)

Cavatini is to the Pizza Hut what French Fries are to McDonald's!

4 cups uncooked, assorted pasta — wagon wheels — spirals — mostaccioli — macaroni — as you wish!

2-lbs (approx) ground round
2 TB oil
1½-oz pkg onion soup mix
2 cans (14-oz each) sliced style stewed tomato
6-oz can V-8 juice
1-lb jar Prego spaghetti sauce flavored in meat
½-cup GRAPE JELLY

Cook the pastas in slightly salted, rapidly boiling water, till tender to the bite. Drain—but do not rinse! Meanwhile brown the beef in the oil in 2½-qt heavy saucepan. Crumble with a fork, browning till the pink color disappears, medium-high heat. Turn heat to low. Add remaining ingredients. Stir lightly to combine. Allow sauce to cook, uncovered about 20 mins, but do n-o-t let it boil! Alternate layers of cooked pasta, the sauce and slices of Mozzarella cheese —or half Mozzerella & half Provolone— sufficiently to fill individual Au Gratin dishes—or small oven-proof serving dishes. Serves 4 to 6.

UNCOMPLICATED

Gloria Pitzer's Copycat Cookbook

SPAGHETTI SAUCE

Secret Recipes

- 10-oz can Tomato Soup
- Half of a soup can Port Wine or purple grape juice
- ¼-cup bottled Italian Dressing
- 14-oz can stewed tomatoes

Put all ingredients through blender, high speed, till smooth. Transfer to 2-qt saucepan, cooking on medium heat, stirring often, till piping hot. Sufficient to serve with 1-lb cooked spaghetti.

MEAT SAUCE OPTION:

In heavy skillet, combine 2 TB oil with 1½-pounds ground round & 1 tsp season salt, browning beef on med-high till all pink color disappears. Crumble beef with back of fork & add to completed sauce in the saucepan.

MUSHROOM/MEATSAUCE

Drain 8-oz can mushrooms and add with crumbled, browned beef to sauce as directed above.

Surprisingly Easy SPAGHETTI PIE — A BRIGHT IDEA

Mix together ¼-cup melted butter with 8-oz cooked-drained extra thin spaghetti, 2 beaten eggs, ¼-cup Parmesan. Form into crust to line a greased 10" Pyrex pie plate. Spread 1 cup cottage cheese over this, then 2 cups rich spaghetti sauce, 1-lb browned hamburger & top with 8-oz sliced Mozzarella cheese. Bake 350F—about 20 to 25 mins or till piping hot and cheese is golden. Serves 4 to 6 sensibly—or 2 to 3 shamelessly!

OPTIONAL STEPS FOR MAKING A COPYCAT VERSION OF FAMOUS SPAGHETTI DISHES INCLUDE MY VERSION OF THE CHEF BOY ARDEE BOXED DINNER.

ITALIAN DINNER
Famous Brand
RIGHT ON TARGET

Herb & Spice Mix:

- 1 packet Mix & Eat Cream of Wheat or 3 TB quick-cooking Cream of Wheat
- ½-tsp black pepper
- 2 TB season salt
- 2 tsp onion powder
- 2 tsp garlic salt
- 2 tsp sugar
- 1 TB dehydrated celery leaves
- 1 TB dry oregano leaves
- 1 TB dry minced onion

As listed put all but dry minced onions into blender. Blend with on/off on high speed about 2 mins—or till well powdered, but so there is still a slight trace of celery leaves in it. Then add onion & blend just a few seconds to break them up, but not powder them. Empty the mixture into container with tight-fitting lid and store at room temperature to use in 3 months.

For plain spaghetti sauce use 1½-qt suacepan, combining in it 6-oz can tomato paste & 2 tomato paste cans of water with 2 TB prepared Herb mix (from above recipe). Add 2 TB margarine. Heat on medium, stirring constantly till piping hot. Spoon over 8-oz cooked, drained but NOT rinsed thin spaghetti. Serve with grated Parmesan on the side to 4.

For Meat Sauce, brown 1½-to-2-lbs ground beef in 2 TB oil in medium skillet, till pink color disappears, crumbling with back of fork. While meat is browning, put into the blender—14-oz can stewed tomatoes, 8-oz can tomato sauce and 2 TB Herb mix (from above recipe). Blend high speed till smooth. Pour into meat in skillet & stir over medium heat till piping hot. Serve over cooked, drained, thin spaghetti. Serves 2 nicely!

SWEET & SOUR SAUCE OR
SPAGHETTI SAUCE

- 1-lb jar Prego Brand Spaghetti Sauce With Meat Flavoring
- 14-oz can stewed tomatoes
- 1 envelope onion soup mix
- 8-oz can jellied cranberry sauce

Put everything into your blender on high speed, about 1 minute—or till smooth. Dump it into a 2-qt saucepan. Cook over med-high, stirring often, till piping hot. Sufficient to serve with 1-lb cooked, hot, drained spaghetti or other pasta. Serves 4 to 6. Leftover sauce may be refrigerated to be used within a week. Or you may freeze leftover sauce to be used within 3 months.

SPAGHETTI SAUCE OPTIONS

To the Spontaneous Spaghetti Sauce, you may also add 1-lb skillet browned and crumbled ground beef —OR an 8-oz can drained mushrooms—OR 8-oz thinly sliced pepperoni, cutting each slice with kitchen scissors into smaller pieces, if you wish. You can crumble enough leftover, cold meatloaf to give you about 2 cupsful, and stir that into the sauce as you heat it.

EXCEPTIONAL
ONION STRAWS

While we were in California last year, my sister, Hazel and our brother-in-law, Chris Allen took us to an interesting restaurant on the Torrance Air Port property, overlooking the landing field. It was "The Air Force Squadron"—where sandbags stacked against the inside walls of the entraceway, and photos of flying heros of the 20's and 30's make up the theme of the decor. The menu is a most interesting assortment of sandwiches and maindishes. But one of their sidedish specialties caught my fancy.

You must use a thin bladed, very sharp paring knife. Slice peeled white onions paper thin—and I do mean THIN! Separate the rings from each slice, dropping them into just enough very hot hot in a heavy skillet, that the oil fills the pan about 1" deep. Stir the onions as they brown, removing them to drain on paper toweling as soon as they are golden in color. Dust with salt to taste and serve quickly before they have a chance to cool off. With ketchup on the side—like French Fries or on top of a salad or to top off a quarter pound of hamburger on a bun, these are especially good!

Make Your Own Mix

SPECIAL

Lasagna

A GREAT MEAL — **FABULOUS**

THIRD DAY LASAGNA Make/Refrigerate/Bake

You put this together 2 or 3 days before you bake it up & use uncooked lasagna noodles. So easy. Leftovers will freeze well in individual serving portions to be quickly micro-thawed & heated within 3 or 4 months.============

Brown about a pound of ground round in a few TB oil till all of the pink color disappears. Then on med-heat pour in 14-oz can stewed tomatoes & 26-oz can Hunt's spaghetti sauce. Heat thoroughly (about 5 mins). Meanwhile put 15-oz Ricotta Cheese into bowl with 1 egg. Beat well. Now – have on hand also:

- 8-oz uncooked lasagna noodles
- 12-oz sliced Mozzarella
- A little grated Parmesan
- Canned sliced mushrooms

Put the lasagna together in this manner:

In pam-sprayed 10x13x3" baking pan, spread HALF of sauce over bottom of pan. Top with HALF of the noodles. Then HALF of ricotta mixture, then HALF of Mozzarella. Then rest of noodles, Ricotta mixture, Mozzarella, meat sauce. Sprinkle Parmesan over top & then drained, canned mushrooms. Seal in double foil. Refrigerate 2 to 3 days. Uncover & bake at 350F- about 1 hour. Let stand 15 mins before cutting to serve. Refrigerate leftovers well covered to use in a few days. Freeze to use in 3 or 4 months. Makes 8 to 10 servings.(Recipe may be cut in half).==

NO MATTER WHAT CRUST RECIPE you'll use, keep in mind that only you know how much crust you want with your pizza. Some like the very thin & others like a breadlike thicker crust, equal to Sicilian style pizza. If there seems to be more dough in the recipe than the prescribed pan size will accomodate -and it doesn't please you, stretch the dough out to fit a larger pan, OR use two pans for thinner crusts. OR wrap up & freeze the unused dough to thaw and pat out to bake an another time within a few months. OR make CRAZY BREAD sticks like Little Caesar's by shaping dough into cigar size pieces. Let rise on greased baking pan till pieces are doubled. Bake hot at 450F- for 10-12 mins or till golden brown. Wipe hot pieces in olive oil & dust in a little garlic salt. Serve with a cup of heated spaghetti or pizza sauce for dipping.

Skillet Pizza

TOP OF THE STOVE SKILLET PIZZA is more favorable to the cook who finds joy in n-o-t cooking anymore than you have to, because it is a 2-ingredient crust! Use an oven-proof skillet or be able to wrap the handle of the skillet in foil to protect it, when in the last step, for a few minutes, you must place the skillet under the broiler.

- 2 cups biscuit mix
- 2/3 cup milk

- 4 tsp oil
- A 12" heavy skillet, preferably Teflon coated or one that has a non-stick finish

---

- 4-oz can pizza sauce
  OR half of an 8-oz jar Prego Spaghetti Sauce
- ½-cup grated Parmesan (Kraft's brand perferred)
- 3 or 4 thin slices Mozzarella (about 3" x 4")
- ½-cup (or to taste) shredded Swiss or Muenster Cheese

- 8-oz can drained mushrooms
  OR 8-oz paper thin slices pepperoni
  OR 1-lb well browned & drained & crumbled hamburger
  OR diced boiled ham to taste

Blend the biscuit mix with milk to smooth dough. Place the oil in the skillet. (Get out your ruler to measure diameter of bottom of your pan.) Spread dough evenly over bottom. Spread 4-oz of pizza sauce over this —or the optional spaghetti sauce—and sprinkle on the cheese, arranging the sliced cheese over that and then the shredded Swiss or Muenster over that. Add the mushrooms or other optional toppings, some you may consider that I did not mention—like crispy fried crumbled bacon or sliced black olives—or green peppers. Turn burner heat to medium high and keep a watch on bottom crust, using pancake turner to lift and peak at it till golden and evenly browned. At once place the skillet 3" from broiler heat for 2 or 3 minutes —OR till cheese is bubbly and other topping ingredients are sizzling to meet your satisfaction. Serves 4 reasonable appetites —OR one teenager!

POLENTA

This is a compatible dish for lasagna and garlic toast with a salad on the side and perhaps a biscuit tortoni for dessert!

- ½-lb sliced bacon, fired crispy Reserve drippings
- 1 cup white cornmeal
- 2 cups boiling water
- ½-tsp oregano leaves
- ½-tsp onion powder
- 1 cup shredded Mozzarella

Let the bacon drain on paper towel while you combine the cornmeal & boiling water in small saucepan, stirring without heat till it begins to thicken like porridge. Spread it over bottom of 8" square pan that you've coated evenly in the reserved bacon drippings. Sprinkle crumbled bacon over top & then dust in oregano leaves & onion powder. Spread shredded Mozzarella over that. Bake uncovered 400F- about 15 mins or till thoroughly heated & top is a light golden color. Serve promptly to 6.

STEP-BY-STEP: MAKING PIZZA DOUGH

PIZZA ROLLS or what Little Caesar's calls their "Crazy Bread" is also like the rolls served at Chuck Muer Restaurants. To re-create these at home, begin with prepared pizza dough from any of our recommended recipes. Let the dough rise, as each recipe will direct, in a greased bowl, in a warm place, till doubled—usually with another bowl the same diameter, also greased inside, inverted over the bowl of dough while rising. Punch down that doubled dough and break off pieces about the size of an egg. Pat out to a rectangle shape, keeping it ½" thick. Roll the dough into cigar shapes and arrange 1" apart on greased and cornmeal dusted jelly roll pans. Wipe the top of each with slightly beaten egg white and sprinkle in Kosher Salt and a little garlic powder. OR instead of Kosher Salt and garlic powder, let rolls rise till doubled on the baking sheet and bake at 375F—about 16 to 18 mins or till golden brown and as soon as they're out of the oven, wipe tops lightly with a little bottled Italian Salad Dressing and then sprinkle in Kosher Salt. Frozen store-bought bread dough can be thawed and shaped as described above and baked into Pizza Rolls as well. There are also small loaf tube can doughs in the dairy section of the supermarket that can be shaped and baked as I have just described, rather than making your own from scratch!

PERFECT PIZZA DOUGH

Make it now, bake it later
ICE BOX PIZZA DOUGH

Keep the prepared dough in a plastic food bag in the refrigerator to use within a week. Or pat it out promptly over the pizza pans & freeze them to use within 3 months.

¼-cup lukewarm water
2 TB sugar
1 pkg dry yeast
2 tsp salt
1 cup Tonic Water
3 cups Pillsbury's Bread Flour or all-purpose flour

In 2½-qt mixing bowl stir 1st 3 ingredients a few times. Let stand 5 mins or till bubbly. Stir in each remaining ingredient, working in the flour with your hands till dough is smooth, elastic and not the least bit sticky to the touch. Shape into smooth ball & let rise in greased 3-quart bowl with piece of greased waxed paper, greased side down, covering the bowl. When doubled in size (1½-hrs approx), punch down. Refrigerate in plastic food bags, tightly secured with wire twists or tape, to roll out & bake within a week. OR stretch the dough with your hands to fit greased & cornmeal dusted pizza pans, so that dough is ¼" thick.

VERSATILE

Brush lightly in oil & dust in Parmesan cheese & freeze in plastic bags to thaw & fill & bake within 3 months. Makes three 15" crusts.

Rolling in the dough

PIZZA FLAT BREAD

Prepare the dough exactly as directed above, but after the last rising, divide into 4 equal portions & shape into rounds to fit greased & cornmeal dusted 9" pie pans. Let rise till doubled. Wipe surface of each with a beaten egg diluted with 1 TB cold water. Sprinkle each with sesame seeds or dust lightly in oregano leaves and a bit of garlic salt & then coarse salt. Place on lowest rack of a preheated 475F—oven for 5 minutes & transfer pans to highest rack of oven, reducing heat to 425F—for another 15 minutes or till well browned and puffy. Remove at once from pans. Store in plastic bags at room temperature to use within a week or freeze to use in 3 months. Makes four 9" rounds.

pizza

FREEZER PIZZAS

Prepare English Muffin Pizzas for the freezer—first broiler toasting, cut surface of split English Muffins and buttering each while still hot. Apply sauce to your liking. Add shredded Mozzarella Cheese atop that and a sprinkling of canned grated Parmesan over that. Then apply canned, drained mushrooms or paper thin slices of pepperoni to your liking. To freeze these, place a half into a margarine carton, securing lid and wrapping 3 times in masking tape. Date each to be used within 3 months. Then you don't even have to thaw them before placing the frozen muffin pizza on ungreased cookie sheet and baking at 425F—about 20 to 25 mins or till bubbly. MICRO DEFROST about 4 mins per half of muffin pizza and then place under broiler—3" from broiler heat—about 3 or 4 mins or till bubbly.

PERFECT FOR FAMILIES

INCREDIBLE

PIZZA QUICHE—Spread thin slices pepperoni over bottom of greased 9" square pan in single layer. Into blender put 3 eggs, 1½-cups milk, ¾-cup boxed biscuit mix. Blend high speed for 1 min or till smooth. Pour over pepperoni. Sprinkle with 1 TB dry oregano leaves, 1 tsp garlic salt, ½-cup grated Parmesan. Bake 400F—about 25 min or till knife inserted in center comes out clean. Spread top with 8-oz shredded Mozzarella & broil 6" from broiler heat till cheese is melted. Cut into squares and serve 4 to 6.

PERFECT PIZZA SAUCE

Depending on the amount of sauce you will use when you make pizza, from time to time, you might freeze the sauce in cottage cheese or sour cream cartons—or Cool Whip bowls, sealing secured lids 3 times around, with masking tape.

10-oz can tomato soup
1-lb jar Prego Spaghetti Sauce With Meat Flavoring
8-oz can jellied cranberry sauce
1 envelope onion soup mix
¼-tsp Tabasco Sauce
½-tsp garlic salt
2 tsp dry oregano leaves

Put it all through your blender till smooth—high speed, on/off—about 2 minutes. Makes about 5 cups of sauce. Divide into family-sized freezer cartons. Seal and date to be used within 6 months.

flawless

Remarkable

SWEDISH MEATBALLS

1 pound extra-lean ground beef
1 cup fresh bread crumbs
½ teaspoon salt
¼ teaspoon ground allspice
⅛ teaspoon ground nutmeg
1 egg
water
2 tablespoons salad oil
1 tablespoon all-purpose flour
1½ cups milk
1 chicken-flavor bouillon cube

In medium bowl, mix ground beef, bread crumbs, salt, allspice, nutmeg, egg, and ¼ cup water; shape mixture into 1-inch meatballs.

In 12-inch skillet over medium-high heat, in hot salad oil, cook meatballs, a few at a time, removing them as they brown. Reduce heat to medium; into drippings in skillet, with wire whisk, stir flour until blended; cook, stirring constantly, until flour is light golden. Gradually stir in milk, bouillon, and ½ cup water. Return meatballs to skillet. Heat to boiling. Reduce heat to low; cover and simmer 15 minutes or until meatballs are tender, stirring occassionally. Makes 5 servings.

Menu Ideas

SPECIAL-OCCASION

THE SMORGASBORD located on Jefferson Avenue in Detroit in the early 1950's presented both these marvelous baked beans and the appetizer meatballs! (Thank Goodness for memories!)

BAKED BEANS

3 cans (31-oz each) Van Camp's Pork & Beans —undrained
3 cans Campbell's Bean and Bacon Soup
1 cup packed brown sugar
1 cup ketchup
1 cup Grapenuts cereal pebbles
¼-lb butter or margarine
2 TB dry minced onion
1 TB vinegar (350 oven)

Mix all ingredients together well in 5-qt oven dish or kettle. Cover and bake 30 mins. Uncover to continue baking 1 hour. If you wish you can place 2" pieces of sliced bacon over top of beans when you cover them—or partially fry bacon till transparent looking and add when you uncover beans. Serves 14-16
(Recipe may be cut in half—or doubled,—accordingly.)

Shrimp A Grand!

SHRIMP BURGERS

Mash 1-lb cooked, baby shrimp with 1 beaten egg, ½-cup dry, fine bread crumbs, 1 tsp bottled lemon peel, 1 TB canned celery flakes, 1 TB dry minced onion. Shape into 4 or 5 patties. Dip in another egg, beaten with 1 TB water. Coat in more bread crumbs. Saute both sides in butter till golden. Serve on buns for 4—with cocktail sauce.

ELEGANT

SKIMPY SCAMPI

I gave you the authentic Scampi recipe above, but here is the way I prefer to prepare it with much better results, via-fast-food-fare!

Open a slightly thawed 2-lb package of frozen, cooked, ready to eat large or medium-sized shrimp. Spread them across bottom of a buttered 10" Pyrex pie plate or a nice looking 9" round baking dish or Quiche dish. Slip them into a 400F—oven for about 5 mins while you pull out a medium sized skillet and place it over med-high heat. In it melt ¼-lb butter or margarine, without letting it get so hot that it might change the color. Keep the melted butter or margarine an attractive blond shade. Soon as it is nicely melted, remove it from heat and stir in 1 TB lemon juice, 2 tsp Worcestershire, 1 tsp season salt, ½-tsp garlic powder, ½-tsp dry minced parsley and 2 TB dry minced chives or onion flakes. Stir just to blend. Pour over the shrimp. Coat pieces well in the butter mixture. Return to bake another 5 or 6 mins or till piping hot. Serve at once to 4.

SHRIMP SCAMPI

2 dozen (2-lbs) large raw shrimp
¼-lb butter or margarine
½-cup oil
1 clove garlic, crushed
2 scissor-snipped green onions
2 tsp lemon juice
2 tsp Worcestershire
2 tsp vinegar
½-tsp dry mustard
¼-tsp season salt
A little pepper

Shell and devein shrimp, leaving tails with the shells on each one. Rinse under cold water. Drain on paper toweling. Preheat oven to 400F—. Melt butter with oil in 2-qt saucepan. Stir in garlic and green onions, cooking over low heat about 3 minutes or till tender. Stir in lemon juice, Worcestershire, vinegar, mustard, salt & pepper. Simmer 10 minutes, stirring frequently. Butter a 9x12x2" baking pan and arrange shrimp in single layer. Bake these uncovered about 5 mins at 400F—. Pour green onion mixture over shrimp. Bake 10 mins longer or till shrimp are barely cooked but tender. Remove from baking pan with slotted spoon and arrange on a flattering serving platter. Serve at once. Serves 4 nicely.

SALUTARY SALMON LOAF

1-lb can red sockeye salmon
6-oz can tuna in spring water
10-oz can cream celery soup
3 eggs
¼-cup dry minced onion
2 tsp bottled grated lemon peel
3 packets Herb Ox chicken broth powder—OR 4½-tsp chicken bouillon powder
2 cups fine dry bread crumbs

Mix it all together thoroughly and shape into loaf to fit Pam sprayed 8" Pyrex loaf dish. Wipe top of the loaf in: ¼-cup bottled 1,000 Island.

Bake 350F— 1 hour. Soon as you remove it from oven, pour ¼-cup 7-UP over loaf. Invert another loaf dish the same size over it and let it stand 15 mins before slicing to serve 4 to 6.

BEAN SALAD — A NEW WAY

Mix together 1-lb can red kidney beans, well drained, a 31-oz can Pork & Beans (any brand)—but do NOT drain these, plus ½-cup sweet pickle relish and ½-cup bottled Italian Dressing. Combine lightly in a pretty serving bowl. Cover & refrigerate 24 hours before serving. Makes 10 to 12 servings. Recipe may be doubled or tripled accordingly. (Do not freeze this salad). Keep leftovers refrigerated to be used within a week.

FOGCUTTER SALAD DRESSING

½-cup Mayonnaise
½-cup Miracle Whip
1 TB Dijon - Grey Poupon Mustard
¼-cup buttermilk
1 tsp onion salt

Mix it all together briskly with wire whisk. Store in covered container, refrigerated, to be used within 2 weeks. Makes about 1¼-cups.

Gloria Pitzer's Copycat Cookbook

HANGTOWN FRY — technically an omelet, comes to us by way of a town in California history, where Hangtown later changed its name to Placerville, after the local hanging tree was no longer used. Traditionally, this dish was served with bacon and fresh sourdough bread.

Hangtown Fry of California's goldrush days, combined oysters and eggs, when eggs were $6 a dozen in the Old West, twice a week's wages for most men, and oysters were as valuable as gold itself. Our 31st state is well known for contributing succssful culinary dishes to our American Cooking Legacy, but somehow, this particular dish remains uniquely theirs!

HANGTOWN FRY

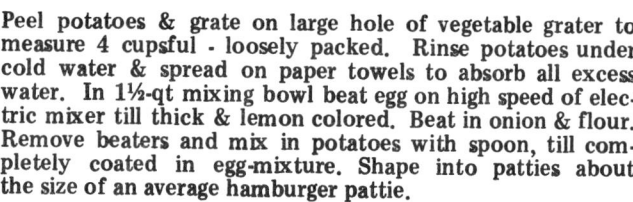

6 baked tart shells
6 slices bacon
1 pint oysters, drained
½-cup flour
10 eggs
1 TB water
Dash of Salt
1½-cups fine cracker crumbs
¼-cup milk
1/8 tsp black pepper
¼-cup chopped green pepper
¼-cup chopped chives or onions
2 TB Butter or margarine

Have tart shells cooling while you fry bacon till crisp & roll each slice around a fork to make a curl. Drain them on paper towels. Then roll oysters in the flour. Beat 1 of the eggs with the water. Dip oysters in egg mixture & add salt sprinkled evenly over them. Then roll in crumbs & pan fry in bacon drippings till golden brown on all sides. Drain & keep warm on baking sheet in 250F—oven when beating remaining 9 eggs with the milk, the remaining salt & the pepper. Add green pepper & onions. Melt butter in same skillet used for bacon & add egg mixture. Scramble eggs as they cook, just till "set". Place eggs in bottom of warm tart shells. Top with warm oysters & then bacon curls. Garnish with paper thin slices of lemon and sweet pickle chips. Serves 6 sensibly or 2 foolishly.

VEGETARIAN CHILI

12-oz can V-8 Juice
2 cans (14-oz each) sliced-style stewed tomatoes
1 TB chili powder
2 tsp cumin powder
½-tsp garlic salt
½-cup (1 medium) chopped green pepper (optional)
10-oz can tomato soup
¼-cup Grapenuts cereal
3 cans undrained red beans
1 pkg onion soup mix
2 TB molasses or brown sugar
2 ribs celery finely minced
2 TB dry minced onion

As listed combine all ingredients in 3-qt saucepan or kettle. Heat gently, medium high, stirring often, till piping hot. Reduce heat to low. Allow to cook, covered, stirring occasionally, till peppers & celery are tender. Serves 6 sensibly. Freeze in small portions to thaw & rewarm gently in 3 months.

U.S. SENATE BEAN SOUP

Into 14-cup Slow Cooker put 1-lb washed, but not presoaked Northern or Pea Beans, 1-lb (approx) smoked ham hocks, 2 onions, each the size of a plum, diced, 4 ribs celery with leaves - Blender Minced (see Index)—¼-cup fresh minced parsley or 2 TB dry minced leaves, 1 tsp garlic powder, or 2 cloves garlic minced and 3 medium potatoes, peeled and grated on large hole of vegetable grater. Add just enough water that ingredients are submerged, to within 1-inch of rim of Slow Cooker. Cook covered on HI 4 hours, stirring often. Then on LOW for 15 hrs without stirring. Freeze in small portions to thaw & warm within 4 months. Makes 12 servings.

SUGAR BROWNED POTATOES

Boil 8 to 10 long potatoes in their jackets. Chill & peel. Cut each into 4ths. Arrange cut side down in buttered 9x12x2" baking pan. Drizzle evenly with ¼-lb butter or margarine, melted and then sprinkle lightly with 4 TB packed brown sugar & salt & pepper to taste. Bake at 425F—about 10 mins or till crusty and evenly browned. Place a few inches from broiler heat just long enough (few seconds) to bubble the surface of potatoes. Bacon drippings may be used in place of butter or margarine for a special flavor enhancer!

LATKES (Potato Pancakes)

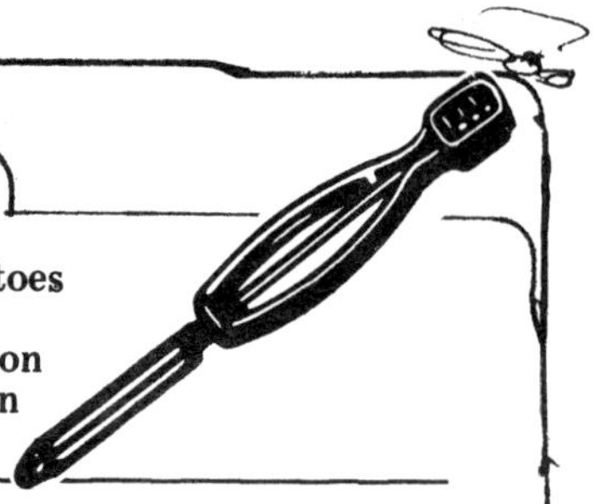

2-lbs (about 6 medium) potatoes
1 large egg
1/3 cup freshly chopped onion —or 2 TB dry minced onion
3 TB flour

Peel potatoes & grate on large hole of vegetable grater to measure 4 cupsful - loosely packed. Rinse potatoes under cold water & spread on paper towels to absorb all excess water. In 1½-qt mixing bowl beat egg on high speed of electric mixer till thick & lemon colored. Beat in onion & flour. Remove beaters and mix in potatoes with spoon, till completely coated in egg-mixture. Shape into patties about the size of an average hamburger pattie.

TO SKILLET BROWN: Melt just enough margarine in equal parts with oil that it covers the bottom of a large heavy skillet, about ¼" deep. Fry patties on medium heat, turning once when underside is crispy and browned. Fry otherside till also crispy & brown.

TO OVEN BAKE: Spray 9x12x2" baking pan or Pyrex baking dish in Pam. Drizzle bottom of baking pan or dish with just enough bottled squeeze-type margarine or cooking oil to thinly, but evenly coat the surface. Arrange patties (about 8 of them from this recipe) in single layer. Drizzle top of each pattie in either squeeze margarine or a bit of oil. Salt & pepper to taste. Bake at 375F—about 30 minutes, turning patties after 15 mins. Bake only till surface is crispy and golden and poatoes are tender.

This recipe yields about 8 patties.

POTATO PANCAKES

2-lbs potatoes (about 6 medium-sized)
1 egg
1/3 cup freshly chopped onion
3 TB flour

Peel potatoes and grate on large hole of vegetable grater to measure 4 cups - loosely packed. Rinse potatoes under cold water and spread on paper towels to absorb all excess water. In 1½-qt mixing bowl beat egg on high speed of electric mixer till thick & lemon colored. Beat in onion & flour. Remove beaters and mix in potatoes shaping into patties about the size of an average hamburger (about 8). Melt just enough margarine in equal parts with oil that it covers the bottom of a large heavy skillet, ¼" deep. Fry patties on medium heat, turning once when underside is browned & crispy. Fry otherside till also crispy. Salt & pepper to taste. Serve at once with applesauce. Serves 6 nicely.

SECRETS

Gloria Pitzer's Copycat Cookbook — Pages 33 & 34

RICE DISHES

SKILLET SPANISH RICE

our favorite recipe

One skillet, and about 35 minutes, will provide you with a very tasty maindish that you can compliment with coleslaw or a green salad and a pudding or fruit dessert.

- 1-lb ground round
- 2 TB oil
- 1.5-oz pkg onion soup mix
- 14½-oz can sliced style stewed tomatoes
- 1 cup tomato juice (or use V-8 for livlier flavoring)
- 1 cup Uncle Ben's long grain rice

Brown the beef in the oil in a 10" skillet that is at least 2½" deep. Keep it on medium-high, crumbling it with back of a fork till all of the pink color disappear. Stir in everything else. Bring it just to a boil. At once turn heat to low. Cover the skillet with a good-fitting lid. Let it cook 25 to 30 minutes, stirring occasionally. Turn off heat. Stir it again briefly. Let it stand without heat, covered, a few minutes for all of the liquid to become absorbed. Serves 4 to 6 nicely. Refrigerate leftovers, covered, to be re-warmed within 3 or 4 days. (To rewarm, transfer rice mixture to greased baking dish or pan. Seal in foil for oven warming at 375F—about 15 to 20 minutes. Or Microwave, 1½-minutes on Defrost per cup of rice mixture & then 1-minute on high.)

RICE-N-RONI SIDEDISH

- 3 cups water
- 2/3 cup Uncle Ben's long grain rice
- 1 envelope Lipton Noodle Soup Mix
- 4-oz can undrained mushrooms

GOOD

Bring water to boil in 2-qt saucepan. Stir in other ingredients. Cover pan and simmer very gently about 25 minutes. Stir occasionally. Remove from heat. Let stand 10 mins covered before serving. Serves 4 & leftovers keep refrigerated, well covered, to re-warm in a few days.

PROBABLE PILAF

- 14-oz can clear chicken broth
- 8-oz can mushrooms
- 1 cup Uncle Ben's long grain rice
- 1 TB dry minced chives or minced onions
- 1 tsp dry minced parsley
- ¼-tsp black pepper
- ½-tsp season salt

CULINARY CLASSIC

Pour the chicken broth into a 4-cup measuring pitcher. Drain the liquid from the mushrooms into the broth. Add only enough water to give you exactly 2-2/3 cupful. Place the liquid in 2-qt saucepan & bring to boil. Add rice & everything else, including the mushrooms. Cover pan. Turn heat to low. Let simmer about 25 minutes. Stir often. Remove then from heat & stir briefly. Cover & let stand off of heat about 10 minutes or till liquids are well absorbed by rice. BO JINGLES STYLE RICE can be imitated by stirring into finished rice, 1-lb well-browned & crumbled spicy bulk-style breakfast sausage and about 4 TB of the sausage drippings. Serves 6 sensibly.

GREEN BEANS SEASONING

Restaurants really know how to prepare their green beans to perfection, in most cases. The Mrs. Wiener chain and the Beef Carver Restaurants have a similar technique that they insist is a secret! The next time you prepare green beans at home do it this way:

Side Dish

In 2½-qt saucepan combine 14-oz can clear chicken broth, 1 broth can of water. Bring to boil. Add 4 TB butter, ½-tsp liquid smoke and ¼-tsp black pepper - allowing mixture to simmer gently a minute. Open 2 cans (1-lb each) Blue Lake Style cut green beans, (Del Monte brand preferred) and add the green beans, undrained, to the broth mixture. Cover and keep on low heat about 15 to 20 minutes, till piping hot, without letting beans boil. Remove from broth mixture with slotted spoon. Serves 4 to 5 nicely.

SIDE DISHES

CHALLENGE

BO JUNGLES SPICED RICE

Another popular request! At home, brown & crumble 1-lb bulk type breakfast sausage in medium skillet till pink color disappears. Pour in 2-2/3 cups clear chicken broth & bring just to boil. Turn heat to simmer. Stir in 1 cup long grain (Uncle Ben's) rice, ¼-cup dry minced onion, 2 ribs celery - finely minced. Cover tightly. Let simmer gently 20 mins or till rice is tender & almost all liquid is absorbed by rice mixture. Add season salt & pepper to taste & dry minced parsley flakes if you wish. Serves 4 to 6 nicely. Leftovers can be refrigerated, covered, to rewarm within a few days.

BLENDER STYLE HOLLANDAISE SAUCE Combine 3 egg yolks, 2 tablespoons lemon juice, ½ teaspoon leaf tarragon and ¼ teaspoon salt in container of electric blender. Whirl until smooth. Pour in ½ cup (1 stick) melted butter. Whirl until sauce thickens, about 30 seconds. Pour over chicken and asparagus.

RIVER CRAB HOUSE SPECIALTIES

CHARLIE'S CRAB SIZZLER SPINACH

is a side dish of fresh spinach that is not over-cooked and so limp you've lost the natural flavor. The spinach is most likely prepared this way:

Take a pound of fresh, washed, well-drained spinach leaves torn into bite-sized pieces. Bring 2-cups clam juice to a boil. Turn off heat and stir in spinach. Cover & let it stand in the hot clam juice for about 30 mins. Then in a 10" skillet melt 4 TB butter & saute ½-cup chopped onion till tender. Add the spinach & the clam juice, and keep heat just hot enough to allow spinach to "sizzle" in the skillet for 1 minute. Season to taste with salt & pepper. Stir in ½-tsp powdered nutmeg. Turn off heat and stir in 1-c Chablis wine (or Rhine). Cover. Let stand 5 mins. Remove spinach with slotted spoon to preheated serving dish. Serves 4-6 nicely.

RED BEANS & RICE
Inspired by Popeye's

Mexican FAVORITE

Per box directions, prepare Uncle Ben's Long Grain rice to yield 1 cup cooked rice. While rice is cooking, use another saucepan in which to heat 2 cans (1-lb each) red chili beans in chili gravy, without letting it boil, and stir in 1 tsp chili powder, ¼-tsp cumin powder, dash of garlic salt. When piping hot, spoon chili bean mixture into 6 small serving dishes, adding a few tablespoons of hot, cooked rice to top of each serving of the beans. Season it to taste with Chili Seasoning Mix if you wish. Serves 6!

FINNAN HADDIE

Place 2-lbs smoked haddock on top of 1 small onion sliced into rings in a 10" skillet with about 1 tsp whole peppercorns. Add about 3 cups milk just to cover fish, adding more as needed during cooking. Bring to boil. Reduce heat. Cover & simmer 10 min or till fish flakes easily. Do not overcook. Transfer fish to heated platter & discard onions & peppercorns, and the milk. Serve promptly

GOOD

BEEF STEW
Inspired By Dinty Moore's

- 6 TB gravy mix
- 1-quart beef broth
- 1-quart water
- 2 medium sized baking potatoes, peeled & sliced very thin
- 10-oz can cream of celery soup
- 2 tsp instant tea powder
- 1 envelope onion soup mix (¼-cup homemade)
- 10-oz pkg frozen peas and carrots - do not thaw
- 2-lbs diced, leftover prepared pot roast or prepared round steak*

*Prepared Round Steak: Cut a 2-lb round steak, that is about 1" thick, into bite-sized pieces. Brown in hot oil in large skillet, high heat, just till pink color disappears from meat. Turn heat to low. Add just enough water to keep meat submerged. Cover skillet with lid. Allow to simmer 20 mins. Add meat & the cooking liquid to stew mixture.

In 3½ to 4-quart saucepan or Dutch Oven, combine dry gravy mix with broth on medium high heat, adding the water & stirring to combine thoroughly. Add potatoes. Allow to come to boil. Turn heat to low, letting cook about 20 mins at a gentle simmer or till potatoes are tender. Add each remaining ingredient as listed. Turn heat to low & allow to cook, covered, stirring once in awhile, for about 45 mins to an hour, or till ingredients are tender. Serves 4 to 6. (Freezes well to thaw & reheat gently within 3 months.)

Oven Meal

SWISS STEAK

- 1½ pounds beef round steak, cut ¾-inch thick
- ¼ cup all-purpose flour
- 1 teaspoon salt
- 2 tablespoons shortening
- 1 16-ounce can tomatoes, cut up
- ½ cup finely chopped celery
- ½ cup finely chopped carrot
- ½ teaspoon Worcestershire sauce

Cut meat into 6 serving-size portions. Combine flour and salt; with meat mallet, pound *2 tablespoons* of the mixture into meat on both sides. Brown meat on both sides in hot shortening. Transfer meat to a 12x7½x2-inch baking dish. Blend remaining 2 tablespoons flour mixture into pan drippings. Stir in *undrained* tomatoes, celery, carrot, and Worcestershire. Cook and stir till thickened and bubbly; pour over meat.

Bake steak, covered, in a 350° oven about 1 hour or till meat is tender. Makes 6 servings

CORNED BEEF HASH

- 6 medium potatoes
- 3 tablespoons butter or margarine
- 3 medium onions, chopped
- ½ pound cooked corned beef, cut into ½-inch cubes
- 1 green pepper, diced
- ½ teaspoon salt
- ¼ teaspoon pepper
- 4 fried or poached eggs

In large saucepan combine potatoes with water to cover. Bring to a boil; cover and cook until fork-tender, about 30 minutes. Drain. Peel off skin and cut into ½-inch cubes.

In a heavy skillet over medium heat, melt butter or margarine. Add onions and sauté until brown. Add potatoes, corned beef, red or green pepper, salt and pepper. Cook over medium heat, stirring frequently, until potatoes are golden brown, about 20 minutes. Serve topped with fried or poached eggs. Makes 4 servings.

BRIEF BEEF BRISKET

- 3 to 3½-lb beef brisket
- ½-cup Lambrusco wine
- 1.5-oz envelope onion soup mix
- 12-oz bottle Heinz chili sauce

Combine it all in an accomodating roasting pan or baking dish. Seal in foil. Let it bake without bothering it at 275F—for 5 hrs. During last hour, baste surface of the brisket in pan juices if you think of it. Serves 4 to 6.

The "flat cut" is the thinnest, leanest section of the brisket, perfect for braising or stewing.

Grand

SALISBURY STEAK

- 2-to-2½-lbs ground round
- 1½-oz envelope onion soup mix
- 0.4-oz envelope ranch dressing mix
- 1 egg
- ¼-cup applesauce

Combine all ingredients thoroughly. Shape mixture into 4 oblong patties, each about 1 to 1½" thick, to resemble the shape of a sirloin steak. Arrange these in greased 9" by 12" baking pan. Wipe top of each in a little melted butter or margarine & dust lightly in season salt. Bake in preheated 450F-oven for 10 mins, reducing heat at once to 325F—for another 25 to 30 mins or to desired doneness. Cut into center of steaks to check for rareness. Serves 4 favorably or 2 foolishly!

BETTER WAY Fast Track

SIMPLE

CHEF DAN GALLAGHER'S GRILLED SOLE
(Village Inn - St. Clair, Michigan)

Dip fillets of sole into bottled golden Italian salad dressing. Marinate a few minutes. Remove from dressing. Coat lightly in flour. Grill till golden brown, a few minutes each side, and serve promptly with tartar sauce and fresh lemon wedges. Allow 2 fillets per serving.

STUFFED FLOUNDER

Two restaurants do this classic dish justice — one is Joe Muer's in downtown Detroit and the other Red Lobster Restaurants, a good national "chain".

- 1 egg
- 6-oz frozen crab meat
- 1 cup finely crushed Ritz crackers
- Grated rind of ½-lemon (or 1 tsp bottled rind)
- ¼-cup finely minced celery
- ¼-cup mayonnaise
- 2 TB grated Parmesan
- ¼-tsp garlic salt
- Black pepper to taste

- 2 flounders each split lengthwise & boned & cleaned, heads & tails removed

Beat the egg briskly and add to the cooked, flaked crab, along with each remaining ingredient (except the fish). When stuffing mixture is thoroughly mixed, divide in half and fill each fish, securing with toothpicks in 4 or 5 places, to seal the seal. Brush generously with melted butter. Dust in paprika. Broil 3" from broiler heat about 6 or 7 minutes —or till golden brown, each side, turning fish once. Cover fish loosely in foil. Bake 10 minutes at 375F—and serve at once. Serves 2 to 4.

BREAKTHROUGH it's so good

a lot of flavor

GREAT POMPOM DIJON MUSTARD

2 c dry white wine (Vermouth)
1 cup chopped fresh onion
2 minced cloves unpeeled garlic
4-oz can dry mustard powder
2 TB honey
1 TB oil
2 TB salt
6 drops Tabasco Sauce

Combine wine, onion & garlic in small saucepan, bringing to boil for 30 seconds. Reduce heat at once to gentle simmer for 5 mins. Remove from heat. Force mixture through fine mesh strainer. Return the strained mixture to saucepan. With wire whisk, add remaining ingredients, whisking till smooth over medium heat. When mixture looks like a pudding, remove from heat. Cool to lukewarm. Refrigerate in covered container for 24 hours before using. Makes about 2½ cups mustard. Keeps for ages in refrigerator, tightly covered.

FANCY

WHITE BAKED BEANS — Kentucky Cold or Warm Bean Salad

10-oz can Campbell's Bean & Bacon soup
4 TB butter or margarine
¼-cup light vinegar
½-cup granulated sugar
½-tsp Hickory flavored salt
¼-tsp pepper
4 cups cooked Northern beans
1 cup liquid in which they were cooked or use 3 cans (15-oz each) Northern beans

Mix all ingredients well in buttered 2-qt baking dish. Cover & bake 350F—for about an hour. Uncover and crisscross top of beans with several slices of partially fried bacon. Return to oven for 10 mins. Serves 4 to 6. Freeze leftovers to use in 6 months. Refrigerate to rewarm leftovers within a week.

PICKLED BOLOGNA

As you use up your sliced hamburger dills, accumulate the remaining juice in a freezer container until you have 1 qt of it. Place a whole ring of bologna in an accomodating jar and cover with the reserved dill pickle juice, adding only enough white vinegar to this that the bologna is completely submerged in the liquid. For 1-qt of dill pickle juice add: 12 peppercorns, 12 whole cloves, 3 sticks cinnamon (each about 2" long), 1 TB mustard seed and 2 TB dill seed, 3 cloves garlic, peeled but intact. Cap the container tightly and refrigerate for 2 weeks before serving. The liquid can be used over and over again for additional ring bologna, adding additional leftover dill pickle juice to it. (Kosher dill liquid is not recommended for this. Be sure the dill pickle juice is one with a high vinegar content.) The spices and vinegar made be adjusted in amounts "to taste".

your own! — SALAMI

HOMEMADE SALAMI — GENOVESE
This recipe was originally developed by Vera Gewanter and Dorothy Parker who authored Home Preserving—1975

Make a mixture of meat that's half lean veal & half pork, the pork being 2 parts lean meat to 3 parts fat. Put meat through grinder with 3 peeled garlic cloves, or allowing about 2 cloves per pound of meat. Then spice it with 1 TB to the pound of meat of prepared mixed sausage spices or equal quantities of salt, whole peppercorns, or powdered clove, cayenne pepper & saltpeter —(the saltpeter will help in both preserving & hardening the finished sausage. If you don't have any on hand, let the alcohol in your favorite red wine or liqueur do the job.) The choice & proportion of spices are a matter of taste, though you shouldn't underdo them, both for preservation & faithfulness to the Genovese way. Now stuff your casing as for a solid, closely packed sausage, following the basic directions in this book for sausage-making. Tie the salami securely at both ends, leaving the string very long on one side, then use it to tie the salami at few inch intervals as if for making a bulky package, and pull each time to squeeze the sausage so that it will bulge (later on the bulge will disappear as the salami dries.) End with a loop by which you will hang it in the usual cool place, per directions in basic sausage making.

The salami should remain hanging at least 60 days before serving it. But not much longer than 6 months or it may dry out too much. Salami of any type, provided it is not the commercially made, that has plastic casings, that has dried & aged a bit may be coated with beaten egg whites all over. When the egg white is dry, hang it again in the same cool place. This should preserve it longer. Or you can age it for a year or so under ashes.

Homemade

IT KEEPS GETTING BETTER. IT'S THE BEST.

SECRET

SAUSAGE — Homemade McFabulous!

Combine 2-pounds ground lean pork, 1 pound ground fat pork, 1 large ionion minced, very fine and 1 garlic clove, ground or minced fine, with 1 TB salt, 2 tsp Tabasco Hot Pepper Sauce, 2 tsp coarsely ground black pepper, 1 tsp thyme, 1 TB minced parsley, 1 bay leaf, crushed fine and ¼-tsp ground allspice. Mix thoroughly and use to stuff well-washed casings (purchase from your butcher) or to form into patties. In either case, pan fry or bake on a rack over roasting pan just till crisp but not dry. Makes 6 servings. Freeze to thaw and prepare within 4 months.

A HOMEY BLEND

Make Your Own

OVER WOOD DEVILED HAM

Sandwich Filling or Spread

Dissolve 2 chicken bouillon cubes in 1 cup boiling water. Let it cool. In this soften 1 envelope unflavored gelatin and place over hot water till transparent in color. Transfer to blender and add 3 cups well chopped baked ham, blending till smooth, with on/off speed on high. Keep meat away from blades of blender by turning off blender & scraping down sides of container with rubber scraper. Meanwhile soften ¼-cup Grapenuts cereal in ½-cup hot water till all of the water has been absorbed by cereal? cool & add to ham mixture using on/off speed again. Add 1 tsp onion powder, ¼-tsp pepper, 1/8 tsp garlic salt. Store in covered container in refrigerator to be used within a week. OR freeze to be used within 6 months. Makes about 1 quart of ham spread.

LIVER SAUSAGE SPREAD

Bake 1-lb chicken livers with 1-lb baby beef liver in 2½-cups homemade chicken or beef broth (or two 10-oz each cans) in covered casserole at 350 degrees for 1 hour or till they crumble easily when pierced with tines of a fork. Remove from the broth to cool. Cool the broth to luke warm. Remove about ½-cup of the broth and dissolve 2 envelopes unflavored gelatin in the broth and place in pan of hot water till it is clear. Return it to the remaining broth. Put just enough of this broth into your blender to keep the blades covered and add 1 cup of crumbed, cooled, baked livers at a time, blending with on/off speed till you have a smooth pulp equal to cement mortar. Repeat the process until all of the broth and all of the liver has been pureed. Then blend into the mixture 1 TB onion salt, ½-tsp pepper, 1 tsp Salt-Spice (in this book) and ¼-cup dry milk powder. Add 1 tsp finely grated lemon rind, 1 tsp sugar (or artificial sweetener or honey to your own taste). If you have leftover sweet pickle juice, blend in about ¼-cup of that or use a fruit juice such as orange or apple or pineapple juice and blend till smooth. Pack it into a refrigerator container and wrap it well. Chill it for 24 hours before using as a liverwurst spread would be used. Makes about 5 cups of spread. It freeezes well up to 6 months or keeps refrigerated for about 2 weeks.

SANDWICH FILLING:

To make a good sandwich filling mix 1 cup of the liver spread with ½-cup salad dressing or mayonnaise (ours or store-bought), ¼-cup pickle relish, 2 hard boiled eggs grated on large holes of vegetable grater and 3 TB dry minced onions. Makes about 2 cups filling. Keeps refrigerated up to a week and will NOT freeze well, so only make up what you will use immediately.

MEATLOAF EXTENDER

The next time you prepare meatloaf, use 3 parts ground beef to 1 part of the basic liver spread before adding the remaining seasonings and ingredients of your favorite meatloaf recipe.

CREAM CHEESE SAUCE

In top of double boiler over simmering water, combine 8-oz cream cheese, mashed with a fork, 8-oz carton French Onion Chip Dip, 1 TB bottled horseradish, 1 TB Dijon mustard, stirring till smooth & piping hot. Serve with chicken or fish or deep fried veggies. Makes about 2 cups sauce.

STRETCHING

VELVEETA STRETCHER

In the top of the double boiler melt over simmering water:
- 1-lb Velveeta Cheese in small pieces
- ½-lb inexpensive stick margarine
- ½-cup grated Parmesan cheese

Stir till melted & smooth and then transfer to large mixing bowl & beat with electric mixer on high to medium speed for 3 minutes, adding a little at a time:
- 1½-cups homemade salad dressing like Miracle Whip

Beat another 2 minutes. It will thicken quickly. Pack it into 1-qt container & keep it covered in the refrigerator up to one month. Do not freeze this as it contains mayonnaise-type dressing. Do use it thinned with milk & heated over cooked macaroni topped with buttered bread crumbs, or stirred into scalloped potatoes, thinned & spooned hot over sliced tomatoes & toasted English muffins, poached eggs, on hamburgers and steamed vegetables. The list of possibilities is endless! (1-qt).

Convenience

SQUEEZE MARGARINE

Beat 1-lb stick type margarine with 2 cups corn oil, adding it a little at a time till smooth & blended.

The margarine must be at room temperature and very soft before you begin—but do not melt it or you will break down the natural solidifiers & will produce a granulated mixture—not the least bit appetizing.

You can keep it in the refrigerator in a squeeze type bottle such as liquid dish detergent comes in. I wash my empty dish soap bottles well in hot water and then soak the bottle over night in ¼-cup baking soda and a pint of water with the juice of 1 lemon to remove any trace of the fragrances that the soap may have contained. Keep the margarine always refrigerated when not in use. Makes about 6 cups.

SIMPLE

BAR CHEESE!

GOURMET CHEESE SPREAD
(Inspired By Farmer Jack's)

- 1-lb sour cream
- 3-oz container Kraft's Grated American Cheese Food
- 4 TB Heinz 57 Sauce
- 8-oz pkg shredded Cheddar

In 1½-qt mixing bowl with electric mixer on medium speed, beat sour cream with grated cheese food till smooth. Beat in 57 Sauce till completely combined. On lowered speed, beat in shredded Cheddar. Store in covered container to serve in 10 days. Do not freeze. Makes about 3 cups spread.

Famous Brand Homemade Unique

SHAM (Minced Ham) LUNCHMEAT

- 4 cups chopped cooked (baked) ham
- 1½-cups chicken broth
- 2 pkgs Knox gelatine
- ½-cup cold water
- ¼-cup packed light brown sugar
- 1 TB prepared mustard
- ½-tsp celery salt
- ½-tsp Salt-Spice (Pg 95 Better Cookery)
- Pinch powdered cloves
- 1 tsp onion powder

In small saucepan simmer ham in broth 5 minutes covered. Remove half of it to the blender with a little of the broth & blend on high speed till it resembles cement mortar. Return to 1st mixture in the pan. Keep on lowest heat while you sprinkle gelatine powder over the ½-cup cold water & let stand till mushy. Then stir into ham mixture. Add remaining ingredients. Remove from heat. Mix well. Pack mixture into greased 9" loaf pan. Chill 24 hrs. wrapped in doubled foil & then slice to serve as you would canned lunchmeat of a similar-sounding name. Saute the sliced meat in butter just till crispy around edges & sprinkle with brown sugar as you go to serve it. Refrigerate covered to serve in a week. Freeze sliced meat to thaw and serve in 3 months.

PARTY DIP Cheese Sauce

THE BETTER WAY

In top of double boiler over gently simmering water, combine 8-oz pkg Velveeta Cheese, 8-oz bottle Buttermilk Dressing (Kraft's), 10-oz can cream celery soup, ¼-cup mayonnaise. Stir till smooth & piping hot. Refrigerate in covered container to rewarm gently within 10 days or freeze to thaw and rewarm in 90 days. Makes almost a quart.

Gloria Pitzer's Copycat Cookbook — Pages 41 & 42

HOW TO MAKE IT
Sauce
Deluxe

Easy-to-do Do-It-Yourself
ATE ONCE STEAK SAUCE

In a 1½-qt saucepan combine these ingredients as listed:

- ½-cup orange juice
- ½-cup raisins
- ¼-cup soy sauce
- ¼-cup light vinegar
- 2 TB Dijon mustard (Grey Poupon)
- 1 TB bottled grated orange peel
- 2 TB Heinz Ketchup
- 2 TB Heinz Chili Sauce

Bring all of these ingredients to a brisk boil for 2 minutes. Stir constantly. Remove then from heat. Allow to cool to lukewarm. Put mixture through blender on high speed till it is pureed and smooth. Funnel into bottle. Cap tightly & refrigerate to use within 90 days. Makes about 1½-cups sauce.

HURRY–UP SALT SPICE

Unlike the version on page 95 of our Better Cookery Cookbook, this is a good stand-in recipe. Mix together 1 envelope Good Seasons Italian Dressing Mix powder and 1 envelope Ranch Style Buttermilk Dressing Mix powder. Stir in 1 TB Accent and 2 TB pepper. Now measure this amount and add half as much salt. Store in covered container or shaker container at room temperature to use within 3 months.

HIGH ENDS 57 SAUCE — *It's Up-to-Date!*
Industrial Strength — *Revised*

I promised you the from-scratch version, unlike the shorter version in our last Quarterly. This recipe should replace the one in our COPYCAT book (page 41).

- 1 c dark raisins
- 1 c applesauce
- 6-oz apple juice
- 1 tsp garlic powder
- 1 TB chili powder
- 1 TB onion powder
- 1 TB turmeric
- 4 TB cooking oil
- 6-oz tomato paste
- 1/2-c dark Karo syrup
- 2/3-c cider vinegar
- 2 TB season salt

As listed, combine all ingredients in medium saucepan. Cook, stirring constantly, medium high without letting it boil, about 10 mins. Pour into blender & blend on "grind" about 1 min or till smooth. Refrigerate tightly capped to use in 90 days. Freeze to use within a year. Makes about 1-quart. (A nice food-gift for holidays).

PEAS & PEANUT SALAD
FAST AND FABULOUS

Empty a 10-oz box frozen, unthawed, peas into a medium mixing bowl. Use that box in which to measure enough dry roasted peanuts that it will fill the box right to the top. Add to the frozen peas. The peas are not supposed to be cooked, and the small amount of liquid that results from letting them thaw while combined with the other ingredients in this salad, is just enough to give it the proper consistency. Next mix together in a small bowl, 1 cup sour cream and 1½-cups mayonnaise (Kraft's brand preferred). Stir in 1 TB sugar, 1 tsp onion powder, ¼-cup dry minced chives (a canned or bottled product), plus ½-tsp dry minced parsley flakes. Pour over peas & peanuts. Stir to completely coat them in the dressing mixture. Refrigerate in a covered container 24 hours before attempting to serve them, which will allow both the peas and the peanuts to soften considerably in the dressing. Sufficient to serve 4 to 6. (Leftovers should be refrigerated, covered, to be used within a week. Do NOT freeze this salad.)

Ala' Carte SECRETS

COPPER PENNIES CARROT SALAD
Inspired by Sveden House

Open a 15-oz can of finger sized carrot pieces & do not drain but pour into a bowl in which you will combine this with 2/3-cup Catalina dressing, 2 TB bottled Italian dressing, 1 TB sugar or the equivalent in artificial sweetener. Refrigerate tightly covered overnight to let flavors blend. Refrigerate leftovers to use in a few days or freeze to use in a few months. Makes 4 servings.

EASIER TECHNIQUE — *It's Quick!*

REVISED HIGH ENDS 57 SAUCE
Better! Easier! Faster! — *METHOD-UPDATED*

- 1/2-cup raisins
- 2/3-cup Heinz Ketchup
- 1 tsp chili powder
- 1 tsp season salt
- 4-oz applesauce
- 2 TB Wish Bone Italian Dressing

As listed put all ingredients into blender & blend high speed, on/off for 2 mins or till smooth. Makes 1-2/3-cups. Keep tightly covered & refrigerated to use in 90 days. Freezes well to use in 1 year. An improved from-scratch version which makes a quart will be in our next issue.

KENTUCKY COLESLAW
It's Easy to Use!

Combine 3 cups shredded cabbage, ½-cup finely shredded carrots, 2 TB sugar, ¼-tsp salt, dash pepper, ¼-cup milk. Set aside. In smaller bowl combine ½-cup mayonnaise, ¼-cup buttermilk, ¼-tsp celery seed, few drops Tabasco sauce, 1 TB dry minced onion. Combine the 2 mixtures, saturating cabbage thoroughly. Cover & refrigerate slaw 1 hour before serving. Reserve 1 cup of the slaw to mix with a fresh mixture on the next day. Use slotted spoon to serve slaw, reserving excess dressing to use on the side if you wish. This serves 4 favorably or 2 foolishly!

Pages 43 & 44 — Gloria Pitzer's Copycat Cookbook

ABSOLUTELY The better way

MIRACLE FRENCH DRESSING

A very oily salad dressing from the Kraft people....duplicated at home is a savings of 50% (77 cents per 8-oz store-bought product).

2 TB vinegar
½-cup ketchup
1½-tsp season salt
4 TB sugar
1½-cups oil
¼-c chili sauce

Put all ingredients as listed into blender. Blend 2 mins on high using on/off speed. Refrigerate. Makes 1-qt.

THE PERFECT COOKED SALAD DRESSING

4 TB flour
2 TB sugar
1 tsp salt
1 tsp dry mustard
2 raw egg yolks
1½-cups milk
1/3 cup vinegar
1 TB butter or margarine
½-cup mayonnaise (optional)

Stir flour, sugar, salt & mustard together in 2-qt saucepan. Put yolks, milk & vinegar through blender few seconds, high speed till combined. Stir into flour mixture & cook, stirring constantly on med-high till thick & smooth. Allow to boil 1 min. Remove from heat at once. Stir in butter & mayonnaise. Cool & refrigerate, tightly covered to used in 6 weeks. Makes 1 pint.

JAPANESE GINGER DRESSING

8-oz Paul Newman's Vinegar & Oil Dressing
1/4-cup Ketchup
1 TB ground ginger or less to taste
2 TB honey
1 TB soy sauce

As listed put all ingredients into blender, or. high ½-minute or till well combined. Keep tightly capped & refrigerated. Makes a pint.

COCO'S RESTAURANTS
In The Los Angeles Area has a House Dressing that has been requested many times by radio listeners.

BUTTERMILK SALAD DRESSING

0.4-oz pkg Ranch Dressing Mix
1½-cups mayonnaise
½-cup Miracle Whip
2 cups Buttermilk

Using electric mixer on lowest speed, combine all ingredients thoroughly. Refrigerate to use in a month. Makes a quart.

Mayonnaise

Into blender put the following
4 egg yolks
2 whole eggs
¼-c lemon juice
1/3 c vinegar
¾-cup sugar
4 tsp salt
¼-tsp pepper
¾-cup canned skimmed evaporated milk

Blend 5 minutes using on/off speed till mixture is smooth. Clean mixture away from the blades periodically and then add:

3 cups oil (in steady constant stream)
½-lb margarine in small bits

Blend again 3 minutes. Refrigerate 24 hrs before using. Makes 1-qt + 1-pt. (3 pints).

McFabulous HOUSE DRESSING
THE GOLDEN ARCHES HOUSE DRESSING

Similar to Coco's House Dressing, you can recreate this famous dressing at home by mixing together the following ingredients:

0.4-oz pkg Ranch Dressing Mix
2 cups Mayonnaise
2 cups buttermilk

Refrigerate in tightly covered 1-qt container to use within a month. (1-quart).

I like Bishop's & Shoney's — BLUE CHEESE SALAD DRESSING

8-oz bottle Buttermilk Dressing
½-tsp onion powder
1 cup mayonnaise
4-oz well crumbled blue cheese

In small bowl with wire whisk, whip buttermilk dressing & onion powder with mayo till smooth. With mixing spoon, stir in blue cheese just to combine. Chill in covered container to use within a week. Makes 2½-cups.

Salad Dressings

WILTED LETTUCE OR FRESH SPINACH SALAD

4 slices bacon, cut up
¼ cup vinegar
2 bunches leaf lettuce, shredded (about 4 cups) or fresh spinach
1/3 cup chopped green onions
2 teaspoons sugar
¼ teaspoon salt
1/8 teaspoon pepper

Fry bacon until crisp in 10-inch skillet. Stir in vinegar; heat until hot. Remove skillet from heat; add lettuce and onions. Sprinkle with sugar, salt and pepper; toss 1 to 2 minutes until lettuce is wilted. 4 servings.

CULINARY TRIUMPH!

OLGA STYLE SALAD DRESSING

My Mother was a good friend of Olga when she opened her very first "kitchen" in Birmingham, Michigan years ago. Her salad dressing —which is a good oil & vinegar blend, has made her famous from Coast to Coast, as well as her special sandwich sauce. My Mother helped me to recreate this lovely dressing.

GREEK SALAD DRESSING

2/3 cup olive oil
1/4 cup wine vinegar or cider vinegar
2 TB water
1 TB lemon juice
1 TB sugar—or 2 packets Sweet & Low
2 tsp dry tarragon leaves finely crushed
1 tsp dry Sweet Basil leaf crushed fine
4 drops Tabasco Sauce
1 tsp oregano leaves finely crushed
½-tsp cumin powder
½-tsp coarse black pepper
½-tsp onion salt
½-tsp garlic salt

Go Greek

Combine all ingredients together thoroughly, using jar with tight fitting lid, in which to vigorously shake mixture while tightly capped. Refrigerate to use within 30 days & shake jar before using. (At Olga's Kitchens, the dressing is measured to use ½-cup with 2-qts of mixed greens & allowed to stand 30 minutes before serving it.)

YOUR OWN

"INSTANT" OLGA—STYLE SANDWICH SAUCE

Combine equal parts of plain yogurt & sour cream. That's It!

copycat

Soup

FAST-TO-FIX

CREAM OF CELERY SOUP—
Use 1 soup can buttermilk to make canned cream of celery soup, per can label directions, stirring in leftover, diced white chicken meat, drained canned mushrooms & bit of onion.

MAKE DO TOMATO JUICE
To tide you over until you get to the store, make a quart of tomato juice by mixing 2 cans (8-oz each) tomato sauce with 3 sauce cans water, season salt to taste & dash lemon juice, a smack of pepper.

Creamy

CREAM OF BROCCOLI SOUP
Thick, smooth & creamy - this soup reminds us of a better restaurant offering, not like Big Boy, but more like Denny's.

14-oz can clear chicken broth
10-oz pkg frozen chopped
   broccoli - partially thawed
1 TB dry minced onion

10-oz can Campbell's
   Creamy Broccoli Soup
2 cans (10-oz each)
   Cream of Celery Soup

2 TB butter or margarine
Salt & pepper to taste

2 level TB cornstarch

In 2½-qt saucepan combine clear chicken broth, frozen broccoli & minced onion and bring just to a boil — 30 seconds. Reduce heat at once to lowest possible point & stir in canned creamed soups, using wire whisk, blending thoroughly. Stir in butter till melted & season to taste with salt & pepper. Then remove 1 cup of the soup mixture to blender with the cornstarch & blend high speed, for about ½-minute or till smooth. Return this mixture to the soup, stirring till mixture becomes thickened and smooth— about 4 to 6 minutes. Serve promptly to 4. (If soup must keep on top of stove, transfer to top of double boiler over h-o-t, not boiling water, to keep warm up to an hour.)

FROM MEAT LOAF!

MEATBALLS —From Meatloaf mixture shaped into grape-sized balls, in single layer in Pam-sprayed roasting pan, bake —rather than fry—at 425F—about 12 to 15 mins, without turning them, till nicely browned. Transfer to baking dish & cover in prepared BBQ Sauce or Sour Cream Swedish-style sauce, baking covered about 30 mins at 350F—. Serves 6

Delectable MEAT LOAF

2½-to-3-lbs ground round
2 envelopes onion soup mix
3 large eggs
5-oz can (small size)
   evaporated (Pet) milk
½-cup quick-cooking dry
   Cream of Wheat
2 cans (6-oz each) V-8 juice

Mix all but ONE can of V-8 together. Save that extra can of V-8 to pour over the baked meatloaf after taking it from the oven. Work all of the remaining ingredients together thoroughly. Shape into loaf to fit a Pam-sprayed 9" loaf pan & bake it at 350F—for 1 hour. About halfway through the baking time, smear the top of the loaf with about ¼-cup ketchup. When you have removed the baked meatloaf from the oven to a wire rack pierce through the loaf with sharp knife in 10 or 12 places & pour that other can of V-8 over the hot loaf. Lift the ends of the loaf with a pancake turner just enough that the V-8 can coat the bottom of the pan also. Let it stand 10 mins before slicing. Serves 6 nicely.

MIX — Homestyle Soup

SOUP STARTER MIX
Vegetable—Beef Flavor

1 c dry minced onions
¼-cup onion powder
¼-cup scissor snipped parsley
2 tsp onion salt
2 tsp Summer Savory Leaves
2 tsp dehydrated celery leaves
1 tsp mustard seeds
1 tsp peppercorns
1 TB dehydrated canned
   sweet pepper flakes
¼-tsp thyme powder
¼-tsp garlic powder
2 jars (3½-oz each) beef
   bouillon powder
¼-cup homemade dry Gravy
   Mix powder
or 2 envelopes store-bought
½-cup bottled dehydrated
   chopped vegetables
....

Mix all ingredients as listed. Store in covered container at room temperature up to 3 months. Freeze 1 year.
TO USE THE MIX:
1 TB of mix is used with every cup (8-oz each) water.
4 TB with 1-qt water
8 TB with ½-gal water
Combine in large pan and bring mixture with water to boil for 1 minute. Cover and allow to simmer 1 hour. Add 1-lb bite-sized pieces of lean stewing beef for each quart of water used. Cover & continue simmering for 3 hrs or till meat is fork-tender.

Great Idea — TECHNIQUE

OVEN-BAKED BACON to use in a sandwich filling—or in other dishes is easily prepared by placing a whole pound of bacon —without separating slices—in Pam-sprayed 9x12" baking pan. Bake at 425F—20 min & then drain off all drippings. separate the slices into single layer & return to bake for another 20 min or till almost crispy. Drain & refrigerate bacon on paper napkin lined paper plates, sealed in plastic food bags.

SCRAPPLE PATTIES
In a bowl combine ½ pound boneless pork shoulder, coarsely ground, ¼ pound fresh or lightly salted pork fat, ground, 1 teaspoon each of salt and crushed sage, ⅛ teaspoon allspice, and pepper to taste and chill the mixture, covered, overnight. Form the sausage meat into six 2½-inch rounds and in a skillet sauté the rounds over moderate heat for 6 minutes on each side, or until they are well browned. Arrange 3 sausage cakes on each of two heated plates, alternating them with sautéed apple rings, and garnish each plate with a sprig of parsley. Serves 2.

SCRAPPLE -Shaker Style
1½-lbs fresh pork are 1st boiled in 4-qts water. Meat is drained when tender & about 3 qts of liquid is set aside. Meat is put thru chopper or minced fine. Bring broth back to boil. Add to it, 1½-tsp salt, 1/8 tsp sage, pinch marjoram leaves, ½-tsp black pepper. Into boiling broth put 2 cups cornmeal, 2 cups whole wheat flour & pork. Cook gently 30 mins stirring constantly. Pour thickened mixture into greased 9" bread loaf pans & chill till firm enough to slice as you would bread. Fry slices in hot bacon fat or oil till browned on both sides. Serve with apple butter. Serves 6 to 8

REFRESHERS

HIGHER'S ROOT BEER

1½-tsp root beer concentrate
(McCormick's brand preferred)
1 cup granulated sugar
7¼-cups luke warm water
(free of any trace of chlorine)
bottled spring water preferred

1 envelope dry yeast
¼-cup warm water
½-tsp sugar
or for sugar-free, use Sweet & Low

In a 3-qt crock or ceramic or plastic container (NOT metal, please...), combine root beer concentrate with the 1 cup of sugar (or use equivilent in Pillsbury's Sprinkle Sweet substitute). Add the 7¼-cups warm water. Stir to dissolve completely. Combine last 3 ingredients in small cup, stirring once or twice. Let stand till bubbly. Add to the root beer mixture. Stir well & funnel into bottles immediately and cork tightly or cap with the plastic pop bottle caps. Do not use those thin walled bottles or those with resealable caps or bottles may explode. The caps should be able to "pop" off if carbonation builds up, without causing bottles to burst. Corks must be tied securely as in wine making. ALSO IMPORTANT: Set bottles on their sides in warm place (70 to 80F—) like near a heat register or top of the refrigerator where warm air circulates from the motor. Do not touch bottles for 48-hours. Then refrigerate about 3 or 4 days & serve it ice cold. Makes about ½-gallon. (Sugar-substitute in the mixture will produce a less carbonated mixture than using sugar.)

ROOT BEER FROM REAL ROOTS
(An old-fashioned authentic recipe)!

For each gallon water used, take 2-oz each of bruised or crushed roots only of sasaprilla, dandelion, spikenard weed. Boil 20 minutes in slightly salted water, as you would boil vegetables. Strain while hot. Add 18 drops oil of spruce & sassafrass, mixed in equal proportion & then allow to cool. Stir in 3-oz yeast & 3/8-ping molasses or ½-lb brown sugar. Let stand 12 hrs. Bottle & cork as in wine making procedures.

SPECIALTIES OF THE HOUSE

CHUCK'S CHOWDER

When Ford Times, Playboy and Harper's all published the recipe for Chuck Muer's famous red fish chowder, not too many people were paying attention—or Chuck was not that well known yet in the restaurant business that people cared. But in the last 5 years it is one of the most often requested recipes from my radio listeners and our family of readers. The short-order version which I developed for imitating this very good fish soup is in our BETTER COOKERY COOKBOOK, but here is the original version. The Canopener Gourmet will probably want to try the short-cut version, finding the result equally as good as the original.

¼-cup oilive oil
3 medium sized cloves garlic, smashed
1/3 cup onions, well chopped
1/8 tsp oregano leaves rubbed to a fine dust
1/8 tsp Sweet Basil leaf
1/8 tsp powdered thyme
½-cup finely chopped celery
8-oz can (small size) stewed tomatoes, chopped
3 qts clam juice—or if not available use Clamato Juice
1-lb uncooked, boneless pollack fish or turbot
  OR use a well boned-lake fish, filled and simmered
  a few minutes in just enough water to cover till tender

2-oz canned clam "base"—or put ½-cup canned minced clams
  in the canned liquid into blender and blend to a fine puree

½-cup finely chopped fresh parsley—mostly the leaf portion of plant

In large, heavy pot, heat oil, adding garlic. Cook till golden brown. Remove with slotted spoon from oil & discard. Do not overcook the garlic or soup will be bitter. You can omit fresh garlic & substitute ½-tsp garlic powder along with other spices later, if you're worried about it. Then in that hot oil saute the onions, adding remaining ingredients as listed. Cover and cook on low heat, barely a simmer, till piping hot & flavors have blended—about 45 minutes to an hour. Keeps if refrigerated & tightly covered to be served within a week. Makes 6 to 8 servings.

SOMETHING SPECIAL

GINGER BEER
(Non-alcoholic)

Mix 2 cups cold water, 1/3 cup apple cider vinegar, 1 TB liquid sweetener or ½-cup sugar, 1 TB ground ginger. Keep refrigerated, loosely covered for 24 hours before serving in equal parts with club soda or carbonated apple drink over crushed ice. Makes Pint.

authentic

Lemon Beer
A UNIQUE LIGHT FIZZY DRINK

1 large fresh lemon
  unpeeled & sliced ¼" thick
1 cup sugar
  don't use substitutes
Enough warm tap water to fill to within 2" of top of a 2-quart PLASTIC jug!

1 pkg dry yeast

Sparkling

Quick Twist

Place slices of lemon in the plastic jug & add sugar and water, stirring with wooden or plastic long-handled spoon or bowl scraper. Do NOT use metal utensil. It causes a breakdown of the acidity so that fermentation will not work well. Sprinkle dry yeast into mixture and stir to blend well. Place lid securely on jug, or cover with plastic food bag, secured with rubber band and place jug in warm spot in the sunshine, preferably, for 3 days—or till you can see the mixture "working" and becoming fizzy. Serve it over crushed ice. Keep unserved Lemon Beer refrigerated to use in 2 weeks. Makes ½-gallon or so.

Official Restaurant Honest EXCLUSIVE

CASINO SAUCE

Chuck Muer's famous restaurants across the country offer this ideal accompaniment to fish, seafood and meats. Especially good with a rack of lamb as Muer serves it.

1-lb margarine
¾-oz finely crushed garlic cloves
½-oz fresh minced parsley
½-oz finely chopped green pepper
½-oz finely chopped pimiento
¼-oz anchovies fillets
Salt & Pepper To Taste
4-oz dry white or red wine

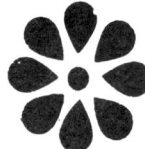

Combine all but the wine in a medium sized skillet on medium heat, stirring till mixture is well blended. When margarine has melted, but has not changed color, remove from heat and stir in wine. Spoon sauce over the fish, seafood or meat. Makes about 1 cup. Does not keep well.

Gloria Pitzer's Copycat Cookbook — Pages 49 & 50

CLEVER WAY

FUDGE ICING FOR GOURMET CAKE

Secret Recipe

- 4 TB (½-a-stick) butter or margarine
- 1-oz square unsweetened solid baking chocolate
- ¼-cup dark corn syrup
- 1 cup confectioners (powdered) sugar

Melt butter (or margarine) in 1½-qt saucepan over med-heat, adding chocolate and stirring till completely melted and smooth. Add corn syrup. Stir constantly till it comes to boil. Boil only 1 minute, stirring persistently. Remove then from heat. Beat in powdered sugar till smooth. Apply the warm icing to slightly warm cake. Refrigerate cake before cutting into squares.

FISH FILLETS

FICTITIOUS FISH

A Spin-Off Of Our "Archer Teacher" Fish As Given In Our Better Cookery Cookbook – 1982

- 3-lbs fish fillets
- 2 cups all-purpose flour
- 3 cups boxed pancake mix
- 3 cups Club Soda
- 1 TB onion powder
- 1 TB season salt

Rinse fish fillets in cold water. Drain on paper toweling. Cut each fillet into 2 pieces, so that they resemble the triangular shapes of the Arthur Treacher fish pieces. Dip moistened fish pieces evenly but lightly in the flour. Dust off any excess flour and allow pieces to air dry on waxed paper, about 5 minutes. Whip the pancake mix with the Club Soda to the consistency of buttermilk—pourable, but not too thin and not too thick. Beat in the onion powder and season salt. Dip floured fillets into batter, 1 piece at a time and drop into 425F—oil in heavy 2½-qt saucepan using meat thermometer—or electric skillet—with oil at least 2" deep. Fry few pieces at a time. Do not crowd the pieces. Turn to brown each side. (About 4 mins per side). Remove carefully with tip of sharp knife—as tongs might break the coating. Arrange on cookie sheet in 325F—oven till all pieces have been fried.

TO SERVE FICTITIOUS FISH DISH—arrange fried pieces of fish in single layer in shallow roasting pan or oblong baking dish. Slice a fresh lemon into paper-thin wheels and arrange in between fish fillets. Add about 2 TB warm canned chicken gravy to top of each piece of fish. Rub some dry minced parsley flakes between your fingers to a fine dust over each piece and add 1 or 2 slices of pimiento stuffed green olives to center of the piece, for garnish. Arrange whole "Broasted Potatoes" in between fish pieces and lemon slices and serve while piping hot. Serves 4 to 6 authentically!

PERFECT

"I'm bored with being a butler!" wrote ARTHUR TREACHER on this 1937 black and white photo from "THANK YOU, JEEVES" movie from which the still was shot for promotional releases.

THE RECIPES ON THIS PAGE illustrate just how using totally unique ingredients can produce an absolutely wonderful recreation of a famous dish, without any confirmed information beforehand of what that dish might actually contain. Club soda and pancake mix in the fish & pineapple in the cake.

FUDGE NUT CAKE

THE NORTHWOOD INN on Woodward Avenue in Royal Oak—during the 50's served a cake exactly like the Sanders Creation—and I do not know if Sanders prepared it for them or if it was an imitation of Sanders—It was good, though—The secret ingredients was a combination of pineapple and chocolate—which makes for an absolutely lucious combination. If I'm going to a "pot luck"—I always take this cake and the recipe for it—because everyone who tries it wants the recipe!

Empty an 18-oz box Devil's Food cake mix into mixing bowl, adding 2 small (or 1 large) box instant vanilla pudding powder, ½-cup oil and 4 large eggs. Drain the juice from a 9-oz can crushed pineapple into one measuring cup and set pineapple aside till later. To the juice, add enough water that you get 1 cup (8-oz). Add to the cake mixture and beat medium speed—6 mins with electric mixer. Stir in ¼-cup of the pineapple. Reserve the remaining pineapple for icing later. Add 1 cup chopped walnuts or pecans to batter and turn into Pam sprayed and floured 10" tube or Bundt cake pan. Bake 1 hour at 350F.—Let cool 1 hour in pan. Invert onto buttered platter.

PREPARE THE ICING:
In saucepan combine: ¼-cup unsweetened cocoa powder, ¼-cup packed brown sugar, ¼-cup milk, ¼-cup butter, dash of salt. Cook on medium heat stirring till sugar has dissolved & mixture "just" comes to a boil. Remove from heat at once & beat in a 1-lb box powdered sugar and remaining crushed pineapple. Glaze cooled cake with ½-cup bottled pineapple sundae topping & then apply the icing. Garnish top of cake with additional chopped walnuts or pecans. Slice to serve 10-12.
Keep leftover cake refrigerated. Freezes well up to 1 year.

SECRETS OF THE BEST

THE GREAT TITANIC & SPECIFIC TEA COMPANY

THE HOMEMADE CAKE MIX will work well in the following recipe for imitating the A&P's famous "Spanish Bar Cake." Because I don't use artificial coloring in my recipes, you will find the cake a lighter color than the store-bought version, but you can darken the batter, if you wish, by adding a teaspoon —or to your liking— Kitchen Bouquet liquid. All things change sooner or later in the food industry, and this very special cake will probably go the way of many other popular choices, but thank Goodness for make-at-home memories like this!

SPANISH BAR CAKE—ALA ANN PRAISE

- 20-oz can apple pie filling
- 4 large eggs
- 1 TB apple pie spice powder
- ¼-tsp powdered cloves
- 18-oz box yellow cake mix
- 1 cup raisins
- 1 cup chopped walnuts

Put the apple pie filling into your blender with the eggs and both spices & blend till almost smooth using on/off speed on "HI". Dump this into a 2-qt mixing bowl & beat in cake mix powder with electric mixer on medium speed, blending thoroughly. Remove beaters. Stir in raisins & nuts. Pour evenly into greased & floured 9x13x2" pan. Bake at 325F— for 50 to 55 mins or till toothpick inserted in center comes out clean. Cool on wire rack in pan for 30 minutes before applying frosting.

BAR CAKE FROSTING

- 8-oz cream cheese—quite soft
- ¼-lb (1 stick) margarine
- 1/3 cup dark corn syrup
- 1 TB bottle grated orange peel
- 3½-cups powdered sugar
- ¼-tsp powdered cloves

Beat cream cheese & margarine together thill smooth & creamy. Add corn syrup & continue to beat till incorporated. Beat in orange peel. Add powdered sugar & cloves. Spread icing over cold cake. Cut the cake into 4 equal pieces. Wrap & freeze what you won't be using within a week. Cut remaining portions into serving sized pieces. Makes 4 bars.

Luscious Fond memories Cake

TUNNEL OF LOVE CAKE

- 18-oz pkg Devil's Food Cake Mix
- ¾-cup cold water
- ¼-cup oil
- 3 eggs

Combine ingredients as listed, beating on high speed of electric mixer 6 mins—or till smooth, thick & creamy. Set aside while you make "tunnel" mixture—

- 4-oz bar German Sweet Chocolate
- 2-oz solid unsweetened chocolate
- 8-oz cream cheese
- 1 TB milk
- 1/3 cup sugar
- ¼-tsp vanilla

Melt both chocolates with cream cheese over medium heat, stirring till smooth. Add milk little at a time & then sugar a little at a time, too. Beat on low speed of electric mixer till creamy, cooking on low 1 min. Set this aside

Grease 10" Bundt Pan with Crisco—and pour cake batter carefully into pan. Make halo around tube portion of pan with chocolate mixture, applying it carefully to top of batter, to within 1" of outside edge of pan, but allowing it to touch tube portion of pan. Bake at 350F—55 to 60 mins in greased but uncoated Bundt pan, but bake it at 325F—55 mins if using a colored Teflon lined Bundt Pan. Test cake for doneness by inserting paper-covered, wire trash-bag "twist" through cake. If it comes out clean of any wet batter, place cake pan on wire rack to cool for 1 hour—or till cool to touch. Invert onto platter. Drizzle with the Tunnel Of Love Glaze

In top of double boiler over simmering water, melt 2-oz unsweetened chocolate, 4 TB butter, 2 TB light corn syrup, 1 TB hot water, stirring till smooth. Remove from heat & beat in 1 cup powdered sugar till smooth. Drizzle this over slightly warm cake. Serves 8 to 10 lovingly!

KATE SMITH'S LUCIOUS BANANA CAKE

From my files this treasured old classic first appearing on page 39 of my very 1st cookbook dated- january 1976.

- 2 cups sifted cake flour
- 1 tsp baking powder
- 1 tsp baking soda
- ½-tsp salt
- ½-cup butter (¼-lb)
- 1½-cups sugar
- 1 egg + 1 egg yolk, well beaten
- 1 cup mashed bananas
- 3/4-cup sour milk or buttermilk
- 1 tsp vanilla or banana extract

Sift flour, baking powder, soda & salt together 3 times. Set aside. Cream butter well, adding sugar little at a time till light & fluffy. Add eggs, beating 2 mins. Beat in bananas. Scrape down sides & bottom of bowl often. Add flour mixture alternately with milk & extract. Beat 2 mins. Divide evenly between 2 greased & flour-dusted 8" layer pans (or a 9x13x2" oblong pan). Bake layers 375F- 25 mins or till tester inserted into centers comes out clean. Oblong pan 375F- 35 to 40 mins or till tests done. Cool in pans on rack 30 mins. Loosen edges with knife to remove from pans. Frost as desired.(To make cupcakes: fill paper lined cupcake tins 1/2-full. Bake 375F 12-16 mins or till toothpick inserted into centers comes out clean. Makes 36 cupcakes).

CARAMEL FROSTING (Like Sanders used to use)

Combine 16 light caramels, ¼-c water in saucepan, low heat till melted, stirring often. Cool. Cream together 3 TB butter, dash salt, 2 cups powdered sugar, added little at a time, alternately with cool caramel mixture, beating medium speed of mixer till smooth enough to spread. Add more powdered sugar if necessary for spreading. Will frost square 8" cake or 12 cupcakes. Recipe can be doubled.

REMEMBER— No matter what the occasion

Cakes Beautiful

PISTACHIO TWICE CAKE

18-oz box yellow cake mix
4-serving size box Pistachio instant pudding powder
3 eggs
8-oz club soda or 7-UP
1/2-cup oil
1/2-cup well chopped pistachios

Dump cake mix into medium mixing bowl. Sprinkle in pudding powder. Stir well to combine. Put eggs, soda, oil into blender high speed few seconds just to combine. Pour into dry mixture. Beat with mixer on medium speed. About 4 mins or till smooth. Scrape down sides & bottom of bowl often. Stir in nuts. Divide batter equally between 2 greased & floured 9" round layer pans. Bake 350F- 30-35 mins or till toothpick inserted in centers comes out clean. Cool in pans on rack 30 mins. Assemble layers with pistachio frosting.

PISTACHIO FROSTING

Pour 1½-cups cold milk into 1½-qt mixing bowl. Dump in 1 envelope Dream Whip powder & 4-serving size box instant pistachio pudding powder. Beat low speed of mixer till smooth & thick (about 4 mins). Set aside. Add 1/2-cup of the pudding mixture to 8-oz very soft cream cheese in mixing bowl & beat until smooth. Now turn this back into remaining pudding mixture, folding it in on lowest speed. Assemble layers with this frosting. Refrigerate cake when not serving it. Serves 10

PISTACHIO BUNDT CAKE

18-oz pkg yellow cake mix
3¾-oz (4 serving size) instant Pistachio Pudding powder
4 eggs
1 cup water
1/3 cup sour cream
1/3 cup oil

MAGNIFICENT OUTCOME

Dump cake mix powder and pudding powder into 2-qt mixing bowl. Put everything else into your blender. Blend about 10 seconds or just till combined. Pour over powder mixture. With electric mixer on medium speed, beat about 4 minutes, scraping down sides of bowl often. Pour batter into greased and floured 12-cup Bundt pan. Bake 350F—55 minutes or till tester inserted through cake comes out clean. Let cake cool in pan, upright, on wire rack 30 mins. Loosen carefully & invert onto pretty serving plate. Drizzle top of cake with 1 recipe of our Blender Vanilla Icing (see Index). Chill cake 1 hour before cutting to serve 8 to 10.

...BUTTER CREAM ICING recipe (see Index) is another good icing to use on the Pistachio Cakes, either the layer cake or the Bundt type. With a neat scoop of Pistachio ice cream to top it off a la mode — you have a lovely anytime dessert!

CASSEROLE LEMON CAKE

3 eggs, separated
½-cup milk
4 TB lemon juice
1 tsp bottled grated lemon peel
½-cup sugar
6 TB flour
¼-tsp nutmeg
Dash salt

Beat whites till stiff but not dry. Set aside. Beat yolks till smooth. As listed, beat in each remaining ingredient. Beat 1 minute on high speed with last addition. Remove beaters. Fold in whites with rubber bowl scraper. Pour into a greased 1-qt baking dish. Place baking dish inside a slightly larger pan containing enough water that it comes halfway up sides of dish containing egg mixture. Bake 325F—about 45 minutes or till golden brown. Spoon cake into serving dishes and top with a little sweetened whipped cream. Serves 4.

CAKE TOP PUDDING CAKE

1 cup flour
½-cup sugar
3 TB unsweetened cocoa powder
2 tsp baking powder
½-tsp salt
3 TB butter or margarine, melted
1 tsp vanilla
½-cup milk

Topping:
1/3 cup unsweetened cocoa powder
½-cup chopped pecans
½-cup sugar

1-2/3 cups hot tap water

Combine flour, sugar, the 3 TB cocoa powder, baking powder & salt, stirring well in medium mixing bowl. Combine the melted butter or margarine with vanilla and milk just to blend and pour over flour mixture, beating on low speed of electric mixer just till combined. Spread evenly over bottom of greased 2-qt baking dish or casserole. Sprinkle the remaining 1/3 cup cocoa powder over top of batter and then sprinkle the pecans over that —although you can leave these out if you don't have them on hand or don't care for them. Then sprinkle the sugar evenly over that. Now drizzle that hot water over top of it all but DO NOT STIR IT! Place in a preheated 350F—oven and bake 30 to 35 mins or till a toothpick inserted through the cake layer on the top comes out clean. Be careful not to put that toothpick into the mixture too far, for a fudge sauce has formed on the bottom during baking and you want to be sure that the cake layer on top is baked but the fudge layer on the bottom is smooth and creamy. Spoon into dessert dishes promptly to serve topped in sweetened whipped cream. Serves 5 or 6 nicely. Refrigerate leftovers to serve cold if you wish, with a scoop of ice cream on top.

SOON AS the cake comes out of the oven, you can drizzle it with a little bottled butterscotch ice cream topping and sprinkle it with some crushed peanut brittle if you wish, instead of adding pecans to the topping as otherwise suggested above.

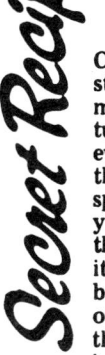

Secret Recipes — *Lemon*

FAVORITE CUPCAKES

CHOCOLATE CUPCAKES

¼-cup oil
¾-cup granulated sugar
1 egg
1 tsp vanilla
¼-tsp salt
¼-tsp cinnamon (optional)
1 tsp baking soda
2/3 cup milk
2 TB lemon juice
1/3 cup unsweetened cocoa powder
1 cup all-purpose flour

In 2-qt mixing bowl, using electric mixer on med-high, beat oil & sugar with egg till smooth. Beat in vanilla, salt, baking soda till well blended. Put milk & lemon juice together in cup till curdled & then pour into batter, beating to blend well. Beat in cocoa powder & finally the flour, beating 3 minutes after last addition, scraping down sides & bottom of bowl often. Divide batter equally between 12 paper lined cupcake wells. Bake at 350F—for 25 minutes or till a toothpick inserted in centers comes out clean. Cool in pan on rack 20 mins. Remove to platter to continue cooling. Frost as desired. Makes 1 dozen.

The taste will delight you.

THE SQUARE PAN CAKE is a mix that keeps for 3 months in the refrigerator, or can be baked up right away. You can double the recipe or multiply the mixture by any amount you're up to dealing with, then when ready to bake the cake, simply measure out the 3 cups for each layer you will need. Chopped cherries are optional!

THE GREAT CAKE MIX CONTROVERSY

One of the advantages of being able to imitate a grocery product at home, when it is just as convenient to purchase the commercial brand item, is knowing that you will have a recipe for your favorite food items if & when they are no longer available. Recently a cake mix was removed from the food store shelves because of a controversial ingredient in that product. At least you know exactly what goes into your own foods when you are able to recreate them at home!

DRUNKEN KINDS CHERRY SUPER CAKE MIX

1 envelope Dream Whip powder
1 cup flour
¾-cup sugar
2 tsp baking powder
½-tsp salt
4 TB butter or margarine
2 TB oil
1 tsp almond extract
few drops red food coloring
½-cup chopped walnuts

Combine all but chopped nuts in large mixing bowl, using electric mixer on lowest speed till it becomes well granulated. Scrape sides of bowl often, guiding mixture into beaters. Food coloring is optional, but will give nice shade of pink to mix. The cherry flavor comes from the almond extract. On low speed add nuts just to combine. Store in tightly covered container in refrigerator to use in 90 days. Makes about 3 cups cake mix or enough for a 9" square pan cake. (Double the above recipe to equal an 18-oz box store-bought mix.)

TO USE THE MIX: Place all 3 cups prepared mix in large bowl and beat in ½-cup milk & 2 eggs, medium speed, scraping sides of bowl often, beating 8 mins exactly—or till consistency of whipped cream. Pour into greased 8 or 9" square or round layer pan. Bake 350F— about 35 to 40 mins or till toothpick inserted in center comes out clean. Cool 1 hour in pan on rack before applying frosting.

CHERRY FROSTING MIX

3 TB Crisco
4 TB butter or margarine
2½-cups powdered sugar
1/8 tsp salt
1 tsp almond extract
1/8 tsp red food coloring

10-oz jar drained & well chopped maraschino cherries

Combine all but cherries in 1½-qt mixing bowl, low speed of electric mixer till well granulated (about 8 mins). Store in covered container in refrigerator to use within 90 days. Sufficient mix for single layer.

TO USE MIX: Beat in ¼-cup milk, high speed of electric mixer for 6 minutes, scraping sides of bowl often. Continue beating till frosting thickens & loses all signs of curdling on surface. Stir in cherries & apply to top of cooled cake. (Recipe should be doubled to accomodate a 2-layer (9") cake.

Do-it-yourself Cupcakes

YELLOW CUPCAKES
Like Sanders used to sell

3 cups cake flour
1-3/4-cups sugar
1 TB baking powder
1 tsp salt
1/2-cup solid Crisco or oil
2 eggs
1 cup milk
1 tsp vanilla
1 tsp other extract

Sift 1st 4 things together in large mixing bowl. Set aside. Cream butter till light & fluffy, beating in eggs milk & extracts. Add to flour mixture little at a time, beating 3 to 5 mins, scraping down sides & bottom of bowl often. Beat well. Divide batter equally between 36 paper lined cupcake or muffin wells. Bake 350F— about 18-20 mins or till toothpick inserted into centers comes out clean. Cool in tins on rack. Frost as you please. Freeze to use in a few months. Makes 36 cupcakes.

AFFORDABLE AND UP-TO-DATE

BISCUIT MIX MUFFIN CUPCAKES

2 cups biscuit mix
3 TB sugar (or use Sprinkle Sweet)
¾-cup milk
1 egg
2 TB oil

Put the biscuit mix and sugar (or sweetener) into medium mixing bowl. Put last 3 ingredients into your blender, blending about 20 seconds, just to combine well, high speed. Pour into biscuit mix-sugar mixture and use large spoon to stir mixture till all of the dry ingredients have been dissolved, but do not overbeat. Divide batter equally between 12 paper lined muffin or cupcake tin wells, filling about 2/3's full. Bake at 400F— for 18 to 20 mins or till toothpick inserted into centers comes out clean. Cool 15 mins in pan on rack. Makes 1 dozen.

HOMEMADE DRY MIXES

Gloria Pitzer's Copycat Cookbook — Pages 57 & 58

BUTTERSCOTCH PUDDING MIX

The few books that I have seen that contain recipes for homemade pudding mixes, usually tell you to substitute dark brown sugar for granulated sugar in a vanilla pudding mix recipe in order to have Butterscotch Pudding. But it is NOT like the butterscotch pudding in the box on the grocery shelves. It's more like pale beige vanilla pudding. The butterscotch flavoring is completely lacking. So to be sure that we have an "on-target" likeness I experimented with various combinations & found this to be my most reliable recipe when reluctance sets in!

1 cup packed brown sugar
¼-cup flour
4 TB Lipton's Instant Tea Powder
¾-cup cornstarch
½-tsp salt

Combine all ingredients as listed, working mixture together thoroughly with fork & store in covered container to use within 3 months—keeping mixture refrigerated. Makes about 2 cups pudding mix or equal to 4 boxes (3-oz each) store bought pudding (NOT instant kind).

TO USE THE MIX

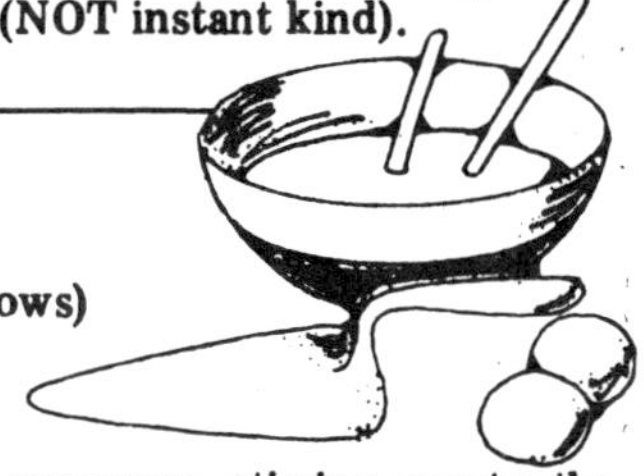

1½-cups milk
½-cup butterscotch pudding mix
1 TB Caramel Coloring Syrup (Recipe follows)
¾-tsp maple flavoring
4 TB butter (or margarine)

Combine milk, pudding powder in small saucepan, stirring constantly over medium heat till thickened and smooth. At 1st bubble of a boil, remove from heat. Stir in Caramel Coloring Syrup, maple flavoring & butter (or margarine). When smooth again, divide pudding equally between 4 shallow dessert dishes. Serve warm or cold. Makes 4 servings. (½-cup dry pudding mix equals a 3-oz box store-bought pudding mix.)

CARAMEL COLORING SYRUP

Combine ½-cup each: granulated sugar, packed brown sugar, water & dash salt in small saucepan. Stir frequently over med-high heat till it comes to boil. Set your timer to let syrup boil gently on low heat for 6 minutes. Stir often or till small amount dropped from tip of spoon spins a short, thin, tiny thread. Remove then from heat. Cool completely. Store in covered container in refrigerator to use in 6 months. Makes about ½-cupful.

NOTE ON PUDDING MIX: When using the pudding mix in the cookie dough recipe, remember that you are using the mix DRY — but to prepare it to serve as a pudding or pie filling dessert, use additional ingredients in the "To Use The Mix" directions above.

FOR PIE FILLING: Prepare pudding as directed above for 9" baked & cooled shell or Graham Cracker Crust. But to the finished pudding as you remove it from the heat, add 1 envelope unflavored gelatine that you have FIRST softened in ¼-cup cold water, placing this in a heat-proof cup and setting it in a pan of very hot water till gelatine & water mixture becomes almost transparent in color. Then add to pudding and pour into prepared pie shell.

SHELF-IMPROVEMENT

FROSTING MIX — VANILLA FLAVORED

Put 3 cups powdered sugar through your flour sifter with 1 cup dry milk powder & ½-cup Creamora powder, ¼-tsp salt & cut in ½-lb margarine till crumbly. Store in refrigerator in covered container indefinitely.

TO USE FROSTING MIX: Remove 2 cups mix & beat well with ¼-cup hot water & 2 tsp vanilla. Spread over cupcakes or one 9" layer.

FROSTING MIX — CHOCOLATE FLAVOR

3 cups powdered sugar
2 TB cornstarch
¼-cup unsweetened baking cocoa
¼-tsp salt
1 cup dry milk powder
½-cup Creamora powder
½-lb margarine

Combine dry ingredients sifting well 3 times. Cut in margarine. Store in covered container in refrigerator indefinitely.

TO USE FROSTING MIX: Remove 2 cups mix and blend well with ¼-cup hot water & 2 tsp vanilla. Sufficient to frost one 9-inch layer.

FROSTING MIX — CHERRY FLAVORED

Put 3 cups powdered sugar through blender with 3-oz pkg cherry flavored Jell-O, 1 cup dry milk powder, ½-cup Creamora powder, ¼-tsp salt, 2 TB cornstarch. Blend thoroughly. Then transfer to mixing bowl and cut in ½-lb margarine. Store in covered container in refrigerator indefinitely.

TO USE FROSTING MIX: Remove 2 cups mix and blend in ¼-cup hot water & 1 tsp almond extract. Beat till smooth. Sufficient to frost 9" layer.

FROSTING MIX — LEMON FLAVOR

Put through your blender 3-oz box lemon Jell-O, 3 cups powdered sugar, ¾-cup dry milk powder, ½-cup Creamora powder, ¼-tsp salt till thoroughly mixed. Store in covered container in refrigerator indefinitely.

TO USE FROSTING MIX: Remove 2 cups mix and combine till smooth with ¼-cup hot water & 2 tsp lemon extract. Sufficient to frost one 9-inch layer.

Whether you call this a pie or a cake - it's rich and quite scrumptious!

MISSISSIPPI MUD PIE

2/3 cup sugar
¼-lb butter or margarine
1 tsp vanilla
2 eggs
¾-cup self-rising flour
3 TB unsweetened cocoa powder
1/3 cup chopped pecans
Half of a 7-oz jar of marshmallow creme
1 Recipe Frosting

Cream sugar, butter & vanilla till light & fluffy. Beat in eggs just to blend. Stir flour & cocoa together and add gradually to creamed mixture, beating smooth. Stir in pecans. Spread over bottom of greased & flour dusted 8" square Pyrex baking dish. Bake 325F— 30 to 35 mins or till tooth pick inserted in center comes out clean. Cool 30 mins. Spread marshmallow creme over top of cake. Spread frosting over marshmallow creme layer.

MISSISSIPPI MUD SAUCE

Serve this peanut butter and chocolate sauce over ice cream or sliced pound cake for a super quick and rich dessert—

In a small saucepan stir together ¾ cup *sugar* and 1/3 cup *unsweetened cocoa powder*. Stir in one 5-ounce can (2/3 cup) *evaporated milk*. Cook and stir over medium-high heat till boiling. Remove from heat. Stir in ¼ cup *chunky peanut butter*. Serve sauce warm. Makes 1½ cups sauce.

PLAIN TO FANCY

Pudding

THERE IS AN ALTERNATIVE RECIPE to the Butterscotch Pudding Mix if you don't care to get involved with making your own Caramel Coloring Syrup, which replaces the additive that is used in store-bought mixtures. You can make up a shorter version using molasses as directed below, but the color, mind you, will not be as bright as with the first recipe using the Carmel Syrup. The powdered mixture, however, can be substituted in the cookie dough recipes with equal success, but the flavor will be less obvious. If you desire a more carameled flavor, then add ¼-tsp maple flavoring to the mayonnaise when you add it to the cookie dough ingredients as directed in that recipe.

BUTTERSCOTCH BLAND PUDDING MIX

1 tsp instant tea powder
¼-cup cornstarch
Dash of Salt
¾-cup packed brown sugar
¼-tsp powdered Cardamom Spice
1 TB dark molasses

Work all ingredients together well, mixing in molasses until it disappears into dry ingredients. Store in covered container in refrigerator to use within 3 months. Make equivalent of ONE 3-oz box pudding mix powder.

TO USE MIX FOR PUDDING OR PIE FILLING

1 tsp vanilla
3 TB butter or margarine
2 cups milk
All of above pudding mix

Put all ingedients into blender on high speed (½-min) or till smooth. Pour into 1½-qt saucepan and stir over med-high heat till you see the first bubble of a boil. Turn off heat and continue stirring till smooth and thickened. Pour into 4 shallow dessert dishes. Serve warm or cold. (It will be a pale beige color but a drop or two of Kitchen Bouquet liquid may enhance the color if that's what you wish. OR for a better pudding or pie filling consistency and flavor, stir a 6-oz pkg butterscotch morsels (chips) into hot, fully cooked pudding, until chips melt.)

VANILLA PUDDING MIX

2/3 cup granulated sugar
½-cup cornstarch
¼-tsp salt
2 TB non-dairy creamer powder

Combine ingredients thoroughly. Store in covered container at room temperature to use within 90 days. Makes 1-1/3 cups mix or 8 servings.

TO USE THE MIX

2/3 cup pudding mix
2½-cups milk
3 TB butter or margarine, melted
2 tsp vanilla

Put everything through blender on high speed till smooth (about 1 min) and pour into 1½-qt saucepan cooking over med-high heat. Stir constantly till smooth and thickened, usually at 1st sign of a bubble of a boil. Remove then from heat at once. Divide between 4 serving dishes. Serve warm or cold. (2/3 cup mix equals 3-oz box store bought mix). This is NOT instant pudding!

COCONUT PUDDING MIX

Spread 1 cup flaked coconut over bottom of 9" pie pan & place 6" from broiler heat, stirring it often to prevent uneven browning, until all of it is golden brown. Cool and put through blender on high speed till almost powdered. Add to dry ingredients as given in the VANILLA PUDDING MIX recipe. Follow Vanilla Pudding Recipe as otherwise directed for preparing the pudding for either pie filling or pudding but also add 1½-tsp coconut extract to milk when incorporating that.

TO SUBSTITUTE homemade mix for boxed coconut pudding mix— (NOT instant), use 2/3 cup of homemade coconut pudding mix for each 3-oz box store-bought coconut pudding called for in recipes.

CHOCOLATE PUDDING MIX

6 TB unsweetened Hershey's cocoa
1-1/3 cups granulated sugar
½-cup cornstarch
¼-tsp salt
2 TB non-dairy creamer powder

Combine all of these dry ingredients thoroughly. Store in covered container at room temperature to be used within 90 days.

TO USE THE MIX:

1 cup (or half of mix) of homemade chocolate pudding mix
2½-cups milk
1½-tsp vanilla
4 TB butter or margarine, melted

Put all ingredients through blender till smooth, using high speed, about 1 minute. Pour into 1½-qt saucepan & cook, stirring constantly over med-high heat, till thickened and smooth— which is about the first bubble of a boil. Remove at once from heat. Divide between 4 serving dishes. Serve warm or cold.

WHEN SUBSTITUTING homemade chocolate pudding mix for store-bought mix, allow 1 cup homemade mix for each 3-oz box (NOT instant) chocolate pudding powder.

Most Extraordinary

PISTACHIO PUDDING MIX
(Not Instant)

Put 1 cup shelled pistachio nuts into paper bag & hammer to very tiny bits. Stir into prepared vanilla pudding mix made from the recipe on this page. Allow 2/3-cup homemade mix for each 4-serving size box store-bought cook & serve pudding mix. Follow vanilla pudding recipe exactly as it directs but when preparing with milk, add few drops green food coloring to tint it light green. Be careful because the heat seems to intensify the color a lot!

Cake Mix

CHOCOLATE CAKE MIX

2 cups flour
1-2/3 cups sugar
½-cup unsweetened cocoa powder
¼-lb (1 stick) butter or margarine
    cut into tiny bits
1 TB baking powder
¼-tsp baking soda
1 tsp salt
3 TB oil
¼-tsp powdered cardamom spice

Combine all ingredients using lowest speed of electric mixer till mixture is consistency of fine gravel. Get your hands into it and squish it well between clenched fists, scraping the sides and bottom of bowl often. Store mixture in container in refrigerator, tightly sealed, to be used within 3 months. Makes 5 cups cake mix or equal to 18-oz box store-bought chocolate or devil's food cake mix.

TO USE CAKE MIX

1 cup milk
1 tsp vanilla
1 tsp light vinegar
3 eggs
5 cups chocolate cake mix

Put 1st 4 ingredients (all liquids) into measuring pitcher, but do not stir or beat these together. Place cake mix powder in large mixing bowl. Make well in center and pour in liquid ingredients. Use electric mixer on med-high speed about 6 mins to blend well, turning bowl in direction the opposite of which beaters are rotating. Stop mixer 2 or 3 times to scrape down sides & bottom of bowl. Divide batter equally between 2 greased & floured 8" or 9" layer pans. Crack each pan of batter, firmly on a solid surface until the small air bubbles in the batter rise to surface and break. Bake at 350F—for almost 45 mins or till a toothpick inserted in centers comes out clean. (Paper-covered wire trash bag twists make good cake testers). Cool in pans on wire racks for 30 mins. Remove to plate and assemble layers with desired frosting. Makes two 9" layers.

APPLES — DRYING AT HOME

You can purchase dried apple slices in the supermarket, and in the health food stores, but it is a shame that more cooks don't try to dry their own, which can be so easily done with the air of your oven.

EASIER THAN YOU THINK! I was skeptical, until I experimented and found just like Grandma used to do, you merely peel, core and slice the apples into 1/8-inch thick wedges. Drop these slices into a bowl containing 1-quart water and ½-cup lemon juice, adding only enough apple slices that they remain submerged in the water mixture. Allow these to soak 5 minutes. Remove slices from water mixture with a slotted spoon, or a strainer, so that the water mixture can be used again and again, sufficient to take care of at least 3-lbs of apples. Spread the apple slices out on wire racks, the kind used for cooling cakes, etc. Place these racks, criscross fashion over the center rack in your oven. Leave the oven door ajar one inch and turn oven heat to 150F—, leaving the apples there 8 to 10 hours. The testing must be with the bite. Bite into a slice or two and see if most of the juice has been evaporated, and if not, let them continue in the oven another 30 minutes or so before testing again. You can begin early in the morning to accomplish this drying process, or you can put them into the oven late at night, before you go to bed, testing them then when you awake in the morning. You do not want the apples as dry as a potato chip, entirely without moisture, yet dry like a prune in texture — soft inside. When all of the slices are dry, store in a mayonnaise jar or plastic (NOT metal) container with tight fitting lid. Keep at room temperature for months and months and months. Reconstitute the slices to natural texture, by soaking slices in apple juice or cider 3 to 4 hours or till plump—or by placing slices into boiling water for 10 to 15 minutes or till plumped. Then you can use the apples exactly as you would fresh apple slices.

APPLE SAUCE — These apple slices are not only especially good in apple pie filling but also when cooked slowly with brown sugar to taste, over low heat, stirring frequently, you can make excellent apple sauce. When the apples become quite soft, put through your blender with a little cider or apple juice, till smooth, using high speed. Allow ¼-cup apple juice or cider for a cup of apple slices. Super homemade applesauce. FOR SUGAR-FREE APPLE SAUCE - use artificial sweetener to taste in place of brown sugar.

APPLE BUTTER is made by cooking 30 cups of apple slices & 5 cups cider or water, boiled till soft. Put through blender in small portions till smooth. Return to cook, boiling gently, stirring constantly & adding 4 cups sugar, 1 cup dark corn syrup, 2 tsp cinnamon & ¼-tsp cloves. Cook gently about 2 hours or till thickened. Freeze in small containers to thaw & serve in 1 year. Makes 6 pints.

AFFORDABLE TERRIFIC

YELLOW CAKE MIX

This is a sure-fire foolproof recipe for an at-home version of the best boxed cake mix on the market. I originally developed the combination of ingredients, several years ago for our 1st of a series of Secret Recipe books, and found recently that the mix was much improved with the addition of the oil and the longer baking time at a lower temperature.

(For a 2-layer 8" cake):

2 cups flour
1½-cups granulated sugar
4 tsp baking powder
1 tsp salt
¼-lb margarine in bits
    (or butter which is better)
3 TB oil

Use electric mixer on low speed to combine the ingredients in a large mixing bowl. When the mix is the consistency of fine gravel, and all of the particles are almost equal in size, store mix in a 6-cup container and keep it refrigerated, and tightly covered, to be used within 3 months. Makes 5 cups mix. Recipe may be multiplied as needed.

TO USE THE CAKE MIX:

1 cup milk
1½-tsp vanilla
3 eggs

Combine these 3 ingredients in one cup, without beating them together, and dump into 5 cups of the cake mix (one entire recipe as given above for two 8" layers). Beat on high speed of electric mixer for 6 minutes, scraping sides and bottom of bowl several times while beating. Divide batter equally between two 8" greased & floured (or sprayed in Baker's Joy) and bake at 350F— for 35 to 40 mins or till toothpick inserted in centers comes out clean. Cool 30 mins in pans on wire rack. Invert onto waxed paper lined paper plates to cool another 30 mins. Then assemble with top-side of layers down, using your choice of icing between, on top and sides of cake. Makes two 8" layers.

FOR OBLONG CAKE increase baking time in above recipe to 45 to 50 mins or till tests done.

FOR CUPCAKES decrease baking time to 25 to 30 mins or till toothpick inserted in centers comes out clean.

BAKED APPLES

Core 4 large cooking apples. Remove about ½-inch of peel around cored area. Place apples close together in 1½-qt baking dish. Into each cavity press 1 TB brown sugar, 1 TB butter, dash nutmeg. Bake uncovered 400F 30 mins or till fork tender. Then combine ½-cup each bottled marshmallow creme & sour cream & spoon over top of warm apples. Serve promptly, dusted lightly in cinnamon to 4 deserving folks

---

THIS RECIPE was only recently an addition to my files of sugar-free recipes, along with the Chocolate Cookies. These are not included in our new Sugar Free Recipes Cookbook.

SUGAR-FREE ESCALLOPED APPLES

3 large green cooking apples or enough apples that when you peel, core & dice them, you can fill an 8½" Pyrex loaf dish with the diced apples

2 envelopes sugar-free Lemon gelatin powder

¼-cup Bisquick
1½-tsp apple pie spice
¼-cup melted butter (4 TB)

In medium bowl combine diced apples with gelatin powder, Bisquick & apple pie spice, coating apple pieces thoroughly. Drizzle with the melted butter and coat lightly, turning pieces with rubber bowl scraper. Turn into Pam sprayed 8½" Pyrex loaf dish. Seal dish in foil, spraying dull side of foil in Pam, placing it Pam-side-down over apples. Bake at 375F—45 minutes. Remove & discard foil. Serve apples while piping hot. Serves 4 nicely.

ESCALLOPED APPLES
Using Sugar

Prepare the recipe for regular Escalloped Apples exactly as directed above, using 2 boxes (4-serving size each) REGULAR Lemon Jell-O powder instead of the sugar-free gelatine powder. Continue as recipe otherwise directs for baking.

APPLE PIE

In mixing bowl combine 3-lbs peeled, cored, sliced apples with ½-cup Bisquick, a 4-serving size box lemon Jell-O powder, 1 TB apple pie spice and 1 tsp cinnamon. When apple slices are well coated in mixture, pack lightly into partially baked (*) 9" pie shell. Seal in foil or place Pyrex lid over pie and bake at 350F— for 40 to 45 mins or till apples are tender to the bite. Cool on wire rack and make top crust by crushed a fully baked 9" pie shell to crumbs & mixing it with 2 TB sugar, 1 tsp cinnamon. (*) 375F—8 minutes.

DAN GALLAGHER'S FRENCH COFFEECAKE

I divided Dan's own recipe by 25% to produce a 6-serving coffeecake. It's best when warm-right-from-the-oven!

¾-cup (1½-sticks) butter
¾-cup granulated sugar
3 medium sized eggs
1½-tsp vanilla
2 cups flour
1-1/8-tsp baking powder
¾-tsp baking soda
¼-tsp salt
¾-cup sour cream
¾-cup well-drained, crushed pineapple

1 cup packed brown sugar
1 TB cinnamon
1 cup chopped pecans or walnuts

1/3 cup hot milk
1 cup powdered sugar

IF YOU BAKE THE CAKE IN the baking dish, containing a 1-lb can filled with dry beans, be sure to carefully remove can, before inverting cake onto plate—or cut it in the baking dish, as you wish!

Cream butter and sugar till fluffy. Add eggs 1 at a time, beating well after each addition. Add vanilla. In medijm bowl combine flour, baking powder, baking soda and salt. Add dry ingredients to butter mixture laternating with sour cream. Add pineapple and beat till thoroughly mixed. In small bowl combine brown sugar, cinnamon and walnuts. Set aside. Grease two 9 or 10-inch ring molds in Crisco. If you don't have one, create one, by greasing a 2½-qt baking dish in Crisco and the outsides of an empty 1-lb size can. Fill the can with dry beans. Place in middle of baking dish. Remove ¼-cup of walnut mixture; set aside. Spread rest of it evenly over bottom of prepared baking dish or ring mold. Drop batter carefully over this mixture, smoothing out with back of spoon. Sprinkle rest of walnut mixture over batter. Bake at 350F—35 to 40 mins or till puffed and golden brown. Cool in baking dish or ring mold 15 minutes. To remove from pan, place plate on top of cake & flip. Tap bottom till cake is free. Place plate on bottom of cake and holding the 2 plates together flip cake back right side up. Combine hot milk with powdered sugar till smooth, in blender on high speed, about 1 minute and drizzle evenly over warm coffeecake. Cut into serving pieces for 8. Freezes well to be used within 4 months.

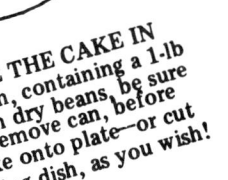

THE FINEST CHEF EASY AND ELEGANT

Our "adopted" nephew is an accomplished professional chef with a long list of prestigious culinary creations to his credit, and we are so proud to finally have one of his secret recipes to share with you. This is the magnificient pie that he prepared on the Jack McCarthy's Friday Feast TV Show in November of '87, over Channel 7 Detroit.

CHEF GREG GARAVAGLIA'S CHOCOLATE CARAMEL NUT APPLE PIE

baked double crust 9" apple pies

2-lbs light brown sugar
10-oz butter
1½-cups heavy cream
5-oz milk chocolate, broke up
2 cups shelled mixed nuts, rinsed

Caramelize the brown sugar & butter together in heavy skillet. Stir in half of the cream, keeping heat on medium high. Stir in chocolate pieces, turning heat to lowest point, till chocolate is completely melted. Add remaining cream. Stir till smooth, & then stir in nuts. Remove mixture from heat. Set aside. Remove pie carefully from the pan, placing it upside down on a cake stand or serving platter. Ladle the warm caramel-nut mixture over the pie till completely coated. Refrigerate pie at least 4 hours before cutting to serve. Each pie serves 6 adequately or 2 foolishly!

POUR CRUST CHERRY PIE

Spread 21-oz can cherry pie filling evenly in bottom of greased 8" square baking dish. Into blender put 1 cup milk, ½-tsp almond extract, dash cinnamon, 2 eggs, 1 cup flour in that order, please. Blend few seconds high speed, till smooth. Pour blender mixture over pie filling without spreading it to cover completely. Bake at 450F- 10 mins & reduce heat then at once to 400F- for another 10 mins or till top appears golden brown. As soon as it's out of the oven drizzle with half of a 1-lb container ready to spread WARMED vanilla frosting. For 6.

GRASSHOPPER PIE

Crush 20 Oreo cookies & mix crumbs (frosting & all) with 1 envelope Knox unflavored gelatin powder & 4 TB melted butter. Mix well & set aside 1/4-cup of it for garnish to use later. Press the rest of it evenly over bottom & up sides of a greased 9" pie tin. Place it in freezer while you prepare the filling.

Combine 14-oz Eagle Brand Milk with our liquour substitute for Creme De Menthe, which is made by melting 1/2-cup green mint apple jelly on low heat till thinned. Remove from heat & stir into it 1 TB rum or brandy extract. Beat this into Eagle Brand Milk with mixer on medium speed. Also fold into it 8-oz heavy cream whipped till it holds peaks when beaters are removed. Pile filling into prepared Oreo crust. Drizzle top of filling in about 1/3-cup Hershey's chocolate syrup that you have mixed with 1 TB rum or brandy extract. Return to freezer. Serve as you would ice cream within a week or two, garnishing each slice in a spoonful of those reserved crumbs that you can refrigerate in a covered container till needed, together with a spoonful of additional whipped cream if you wish. This pie serves 8 adequately or 2 foolishly. Keep frozen.

DO-IT-YOURSELF FOR GROCERIES!

TO THE RESCUE

CHOCOLATE PUDDING - From Scratch

3-oz solid unsweetened baking chocolate	6 TB flour
3 cups milk	¼-tsp salt
Scant cup of sugar (or 2 TB Sweet 10)	1 tsp vanilla

In top of double boiler over gently simmering water, combine chocolate with 2 cups of the milk. Put the remaining cup of milk into blender with sugar, flour & salt. Blend on high speed till absolutely smooth. Stir this into hot milk-chocolate mixture, stirring till chocolate has completely melted and mixture begins to thicken and become smooth. Allow to cook over the gently simmering water for 10 minutes, stirring often. Add vanilla and divide between 6 dessert dishes. Serve warm or chilled.

FRENCH SILK PIE

Have a 9" fully baked pie shell well chilled and handy. Prepare the Chocolate Pudding per recipe above, and as soon as you add the vanilla, without removing it from over the simmering water, also stir in a 6-oz pkg semi-sweet chocolate morsels. Stir till chocolate melts. In a small measuring cup, containing ¼-cup cold water, sprinkle in 1 envelope Knox unflavored gelatine powder till mushy. Stir Knox mixture into hot pudding mixture. Stir well to be sure it dissolves completely. Pour into chilled pie shell, only till pudding mixture comes to rim of shell. Refrigerate filled pie and any leftover pie filling about an hour and then pile remaining filling artistically over top of filled pie, mounding it nicely. Chill several hours, or overnight before cutting to serve 6. Garnish each serving in whipped cream & a Hershey bar shaved with a potato peeler into nice little curls. Serves 6.

BREAD PUDDING

14-oz can Eagle Brand Milk
3 cups hot water
2 cups crumbled stale white bread
3 eggs - beaten
2 TB butter or margarine—melted
½-tsp salt
1 tsp vanilla
Dash nutmeg

Combine Eagle Brand & hot water stirring till smooth. Add bread to this and set aside for 10 mins. Then stir in remaining ingredients. Pour into greased 1½-qt baking dish. Place in slightly larger pan containing enough water that it comes halfway up sides of dish containing bread pudding. Bake 350F—for 1 hour. Or till knife inserted in center comes out clean. Serve warm or cold. Serves 6. (Refrigerate leftovers to rewarm within 3 days.)

SPECULATION SPANISH CREAM

1 envelope unflavored gelatin
¼-cup cold water
2 pkgs (3-oz each) instant vanilla pudding
3 cups cold milk
8-oz carton Cool Whip - thawed

GOOD

Soften gelatin in cold water. Place in heat-proof cup & set it in a pan of hot water till transparent. Combine pudding powder with the 3 cups milk in blender on high speed till smooth. Turn off motor and pour in gelatin mixture. Blend again a few seconds. Pour into mixing bowl. Let stand 5 minutes or till thickened. Fold in Cool Whip. Pour into lightly oiled 1½-qt mold. Chill till firm enough to unmold onto serving place. Garnish with additional Cool Whip. Serves 6.

FLOATING ISLAND

Prepare the Spanish Cream but divide the Cream between 8 lightly oiled 6-oz Pyrex custard cups. Chill till firm. Unmold each into dessert dish. Spoon slightly sweetened, frozen, but thawed sliced strawberries over each inverted cup of Cream. OR drizzle with chocolate syrup and top with peanuts—and/or Cool Whip. Serves 8

HOT BUTTERSCOTCH

Again, like the "Hot Fudge" recipe in the top of a double boiler over simmering water combine:
- 12-oz pkg Butterscotch Chips
- 14-oz can Eagle Brand Milk
- 14-oz light corn syrup (using milk can to measure this)
- ½-lb butter or margarine
- Dash of Salt
- 12 light Kraft Caramels

Cooking & stirring till smooth & then continuing to let it cook without stirring for 30 mins. Beat with electric mixer on high speed for 5 minutes and then add 1 tsp maple flavoring, beating another minute or two. Store in covered container in refrigerator up to 30 days. Makes about a quart.

WATERGATE CAKE

- 18-oz pkg yellow cake mix
- ¾-cup corn oil
- 3 eggs
- 8-oz 7-UP or Sprite
- 3½-oz pkg pistachio instant pudding powder
- 1 c chopped walnuts or pecans
- ½-c shredded coconut

Secretly combine all ingredients as listed, beating confidentially until well-blended. Pour into a greased & floured 9x12x2-inch cake pan. Bake discreetly for 45 min at 350 degrees. Let cool 1 hour before frosting the cake.

COVER-UP ICING

- 2 envelopes Dream Whip powder used dry
- 1½-cups ice-cold milk
- 3½-oz pkg instant pistachio pudding powder
- ½-cup shredded coconut
- ¾-c chopped walnuts or pecan

Your mission--if you should decide to accept it--is to combine all icing ingredients as listed in a deep but small mixing bowl & sufficiently agitate these with an electric mixer on high speed until mixture is smooth. Sufficient to ice a 9x12x2-inch cake.

THE SECRET

WATERGATE CAKE AND COVER-UP ICING — SPECIAL

THE REPUBLICAN CONVENTION was in Detroit on one of those Monday mornings when Dave Lockhart called me for a recipe and restaurant chat over WXYZ. I didn't think they would ever call me again after the surprise I gave them that morning, but within a few days a certficate of appreciation, gold border and all, arrived in the mail for the contribution I had made to the spirit of the Republican Convention.

When Dave Lockhart said his cheerful "Good Morning"—and there was that pause that gave me my cue to respond I came back with the following dialogue...."Mr. Chairman....Mr. Chairman! The deligate from St. Clair wishes to be recognized.....Mr. Chairman, the great community of St. Clair, home of the Blue Water Festival, world headquarters of the Diamond Crystal Salt Company and sunshine and sustenance would like to——" Dave came back with one of those uncontrollable chuckles of astonishment and agreed to recognize "the deligate from St. Clair.".......'"Mr. Chairman," I went on..."would the ushers please clear the aisles. The aisles must be cleared. Ushers, move those deligates out of the aisles, pullease..." (There was laughter from the radio studio as Dave picked up on it, and asked that those aisles be cleared....) "Will the deligate with the lamp shade on his head please return it to the hospitality room?" I continued. And finally we came to what recipe I had selected for the day.

"The Watergate Cake & Cover-Up Icing," I assured him. And went on to give the recipe with the endorsement that St. Clair had cast all of its 3½ votes for this dark horse candidate in the dessert category of the political race for a fast and easy vote-getter.

THE CAKE

Mix together and set aside: 2 cups flour, 2 cups sugar. In small saucepan bring to a boil——1 cup water, 1 cup corn oil, ¼-cup unsweetened cocoa powder. Stir till smooth, allowing it to boil gently about half a minute. Remove at once from heat and immediately pour it over the flour-sugar and beat with portable electric mixer on medium speed to a smooth batter. Beat in 2 eggs, 1/3 cup buttermilk, 1 tsp vanilla, 1 tsp baking soda and a pinch of salt. Beat 3 minutes on medium-high speed. Pour it into a greased jelly roll pan (11x17x1") and bake at 375F—about 20 minutes or till a toothpick inserted in center comes out clean. Meanwhile prepare the icing.

THE ICING

In 1½-qt saucepan over medium heat combine ½-lb (2 sticks) margarine or butter, ¼-cup unsweetened cocoa powder, 1/3 cup whole milk, ¼-cup packed brown sugar, dash of salt. Stir constantly till smooth and bring to a boil. Let it boil only a minute while stirring vigorously. Remove from heat and beat in 1-lb powdered sugar, 1 TB vanilla and ¼-lb additional butter or margarine, quite soft, beating to a spreading consistency. Remove beaters and stir in 1 cup chopped walnuts or pecans. Return the icing to lowest possible heat, just to keep it warm, or place in top of double boiler over hot water, to be sure it will not scorch. Then as soon as the cake is out of the oven, place the cake pan on a wire rack, and at once pour the warm frosting over the hot cake. It will fall—It's supposed to! The final result when cake cools completely is a fudgy, custard-like consistency under a smooth, rich fudgy icing. Cut into squares and serve as you would brownies. Keep refrigerated and covered to be served within a week. The cake freezes well to be used within 6 months. Serves 8 to 10 deligates.

Scrumpshus!

DREARY QUEEN HOT FUDGE

- 6 Milky Way candy bars (2.1-oz each)
- 12-oz pkg milk chocolate morsels
- 5.3-oz (small) PET MILK
- ½-lb butter (2 sticks)

Put everything into top of double boiler & stir over simmering water till smooth & completely melted (about 20 mins). Cook without stirring another 20 mins. Beat with electric mixer - high speed till smooth & store in 1-qt container, tightly covered, refrigerated to use within a month. Freeze to use within 6 months. Makes about a quart.

BASKET & RIBBONS CHOCOLATE SYRUP

- 2 TB light corn syrup
- Dash of Salt
- ½-cup Hershey's cocoa powder
- 1 cup granulated sugar
- 1 cup packed brown sugar
- 1 cup hot water

Bring everything to boil, stirring constantly, in 1½-qt saucepan, over medium-high heat. At 1st sign of boil reduce heat to gentle simmer & continue to stir — 3 minutes. Remove from heat. Add a tspful vanilla if you wish. Cool & store in covered container, refrigerated. (3 cups).

HOT CARAMEL SAUCE

- 1¼-cup packed brown sugar
- 2/3 cup light corn syrup
- 2/3 cup heavy cream
- 4 TB butter or margarine
- Dash of Salt
- ½-tsp vanilla

Combine everything but vanilla in 1½-qt saucepan. Cook & stir constantly over medium-high to the "soft ball stage"—just as you would if making fudge. (About 238F—on a candy thermometer.) Cool slightly and stir in vanilla. Serve it lukewarm spooned over ice cream. Makes about 2 cups. Keep leftover sauce refrigerated in covered container to be used within a month.

Candies

MOLASSES TAFFY

14-oz can Eagle Brand Milk
½-cup light molasses
Dash of salt

In heavy 2½-qt saucepan combine the 3 ingredients and cook, stirring constantly, medium-high till mixture reaches 245F—on candy thermometer (firm ball stage)—about 20 to 22 minutes.

Remove from heat & pour candy into Pam-sprayed 9" square baking pan. Let cool on rack till you can handle it. Wipe your hands with butter and pull mixture — stretching it till becomes light in color and shiny. Twist the candy into a long rope, about ¾" thick, snipping it off into 1" pieces with Pam-sprayed scissors. Wrap each piece in square of plastic wrap. Store candy in lightly covered containers at room temperature to use in about a month. Makes about 50 pieces.

CARAMELS

1 cup sugar
1 cup heavy cream
3 TB light Karo syrup
2 TB butter or margarine
1 tsp vanilla extract

In heavy 2½-qt saucepan combine all but vanilla on medium-high heat, stirring constantly till comes to a boil & sugar is completely dissolved. Place a candy thermometer on side of pan so that bulb touches bottom of mixture in pan & cook the candy, without stirring, medium-high, till temperature reaches 245F—(firm ball stage—when small amount dropped into cup cold water forms firm ball)—about 30 minutes. Remove from heat. Stir in vanilla. Pour mixture into Pam-sprayed 9" square baking metal pan—NOT glass as it might crack from heat of candy! Cool candy in pan on rack 30 mins. Cut candy into ½-" by 2" pieces. Wrap each in a square of plastic wrap. Store in tightly covered air-tight container at room temperature to serve within a month. Makes 64 pieces.

Easy-to-Make

HOMEMADE RAISINS

Choose white muscat or seedless grapes, discarding any that are not perfect. Bring to boil 1 TB baking soda & 1-qt water. Put cupful of grapes at a time into strainer with a handle & lower into solution, as it simmering gently, for only 30 seconds. Spread on brown paper lined baking sheets to dry in sun or 150F—oven 12 to 15 hours or till moisture all evaporates. Store in covered container, refrigerated. 1-lb grapes yields ½-lb raisins.

SOMETHING DIFFERENT

JORDASH ALMONDS

2-2/3 cups sugar
½-cup water
1 tsp powdered cardamom
3 cups unblanched almonds

Stir sugar & water in 2-qt heavy saucepan over med-heat, till sugar dissolves. Add cardamom powder. Boil briskly till mixture falls from tip of spoon in thick drops. Add almonds, coating them thoroughly in sugar mixture. Remove pan from heat but keep on stirring mixture till sugar clings to almonds and dries into a sugary substance. Put mixture into strainer & shake to remove excess sugar, catching it in pan below. Add few drops water to it & return to heat to melt if needed to recoat nuts.

GUMDROPS

6-oz liquid pectin
¼-tsp baking soda
¾-cup sugar
¾-cup light Karo syrup
2 tsp any flavor extract
¼-tsp any color food coloring
Sugar in which to coat candy

Combine pectin & soda in 1½-qt saucepan. It will foam. Mix sugar & Karo in 2-qt saucepan & cook it gently, stirring frequently. At same time put the pectin & soda over heat until foam subsides. Remove this from heat. Continue cooking sugar & corn syrup till it comes to boil. Boil briskly 4 or 5 mins. Now pour the hot pectin mixture into boiling sugar mixture, stirring constantly as you do. Let mixture boil about 10 seconds. Remove from heat. Add extract of your choice & a compatible color of food coloring. At once pour into lightly oiled 8" square pan. Cool at room temperature 2 or 3 hrs or till firm. Use a greased large thimble to cut out pieces from solid mixture — or cut into small shapes & coat in sugar. Refrigerate to use within a month. Makes about 3 dozen pieces.

Nostalgic

Brown's Hot Fudge
MEMORIES OF HOT FUDGE!

REMEMBER BROWN'S CREAMERY of Royal Oak-Detroit area in the 50's and you'll recall their special topping for ice cream. In competition at that time with Sanders, Brown's did a good job, considering that they only had 2 outlets and Sanders had dozens of stores. Sanders really has no competition, and while I prefer Sanders for texture and flavor (see Fast Food Book pages 62 - 78) this is worth adding to your reliable recipe files.

8-oz sour cream
¼-lb (1 stick) butter or margarine
2/3 cup dark corn syrup (Karo)
½-cup firmly packed
 light brown sugar

6 Nestles milk chocolate candy bars
 each 1.45-oz & in red & white wrappers

1 tsp vanilla

Put all but vanilla into top of double boiler over gently simmering water. Stir till smooth & ingredients are completely melted. Allow to cook without stirring, over that gently simmering water, for 45 minutes. Put hot fudge mixture through blender, adding the vanilla, high speed, about 20 seconds, or till completely smooth. Pour into refrigerator container with tight fitting lid. Rewarm over hot water or on "defrost" in Microwave, to serve over ice cream. Makes about 2 cups. Use within 2 weeks or freeze to thaw & use in 6 months. Serves 6 sensibly or 2 without any sense of reason!

LOLLIPOPS

HONEY SUCKLE SUCKERS

1 cup sugar
¼-cup light corn syrup
¼-cup honey
¼-cup hot water
Dash Salt

In 2½-qt saucepan, combine all ingredients, bringing mixture to a full hard boil, stirring constantly. At once turn heat down so that mixture just barely bubbles above a low simmer. Set timer for 12 mins & let it cook without stirring for that long. Remove from heat. Drop in:
 2 TB margarine
 ½ tsp orange extract
Stir thoroughly till margarine has melted & becomes incorporated into candy mixture. At once drop by tablespoonful onto Pam-sprayed cookie sheets on which you have spaced flat wooden poocicle sticks. Be sure you drop the hot candy in such a way that it covers one end of each stick. Allow to harden at room temperature about 1 hour. Wrap & store —Makes 1 dozen.

AS HARD CANDIES—drop mixture into Pam-sprayed miniature muffin wells or thimble sized molds. Allow to harden. Remove from olds. Wrap & store.

OLD FASHIONED CANDY
 Pour hot candy mixture into Pam-sprayed jelly roll pan. As soon as you can handle the warm candy (not letting it cool too much)—take Pam-sprayed kitchen scissors and snip into bite-sized pieces, pulling mixture into ribbon like pieces. Dust in powdered sugar and store in glass containers.

STEP-BY-STEP: Pie Shell

BUTTER CRUST

This is the one very special recipe that I always repeat in every one of my publications and my books, because it is the only pie crust recipe I use and don't want you to have to turn elsewhere to look it up. It's simple, rich, fool-proof and you do not have to use a rolling pin!

¼-lb butter
1 cup flour
1 TB sugar
½-tsp salt
Dash of cinnamon

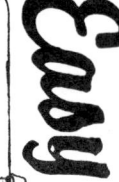

Melt the butter. Pour it into a 1½-qt, deep, narrow mixing bowl. Dump in the other ingredients all at once. Beat on high speed 30-seconds with electric mixer. The mixture will leave the center of the bowl and cling to the sides of the bowl — at which point, you remove the beaters. Quickly gather the still warm dough into a crude ball & pat it out quickly over a Pam-sprayed 9-or-10-inch Pyrex pie plate or metal pie pan. Pat it up the sides to the rim and evenly over the bottom. Do not prick it with a fork as you might ordinarily do for another crust. Bake it completely at 375F— for 22 mins or till golden brown. It's then ready to fill with a non-bake filling.

When you are using a filling that must be baked in a crust, PARTIALLY bake the bottom crust, empty, at 375F—for 12 mins. Then fill it and bake per filling directions for time and temperature.

SLOVAKIAN NUT CANDY

In 10-inch skillet, heat and stir 1 cup granulated sugar till melted and golden brown. Stir in 1 cup finely chopped pecans, 1 teaspoon vanilla, and ⅛ teaspoon salt. Pour immediately onto buttered board or baking sheet. Roll quickly with buttered rolling pin to 8x8x¼-inch square. Quickly cut into diamonds. Makes ½ pound.

Remarkable ROCK CANDY

This is an old fashioned formula for an old fashioned favorite that is fun to make, but takes about 5 to 6 weeks. I have never found, in all of my files, a recipe equal to this, nor even similar. If you're patient, it will work but it does take time.

(1) Lukewarm water in a jar to within an inch from top.

(2) Add enough sugar to make a honey-like consistency.

(3) Put in a string so that it doesn't touch bottom and string is tied to a pencil at top to keep from falling into jar.

(4) Drop string in and set aside till it crystalizes, removing that amount, leaving candy on string, and replacing with fresh string, repeating till sugar mixture coats string in rocklike pieces.

VELVEETA FUDGE Extraordinaire

Whenever I visit Niagara Falls, Ontario, I always enjoy the wonderful fudge shops in the Maple Leaf Village. The only combination of ingredients that I have ever found that produces an identical result to Niagara Fudge is this recipe, of which, the secret ingredient for the smooth texture, turns out to be Velveeta Cheese. The fudge in its final state, however, has absolutely no trace of a cheese flavor or taste.

½-lb Velveeta Cheese — in 10 or 12 pinched off pieces
½-lb (2 sticks) butter or margarine
½-cup unsweetened cocoa powder
2-lbs powdered sugar
2 tsp vanilla extract

In top of double boiler, over gently simmering water, combine cheese, butter, cocoa powder, stirring occasionally until completely melted & smooth. With portable electric mixer, while still over hot water, beat in a cup of the powdered sugar, then the vanilla, and finally the remaining powdered sugar in small portions until smooth & thickened. Pour fudge at once into buttered or Pam-sprayed 9x9x2 pan for thick squares—or into Pam-sprayed 9x12x2" pan for thin squares. Chill several hours before cutting into squares.

MADE SIMPLE

FOR A 2-CRUST PIE:
Prepare 2 crusts, as directed in recipe (at left), but completely bake one of the crusts. When it's cooled, crumble it up into fine crumbs and mix it with 1 TB sugar & 1 tsp cinnamon. Sprinkle it evenly over top of baked & filled fruit pies — such as cherry, blueberry, raspberry or peach pies. Prepare the pie per filling recipe directions, baking in accordance with time & temperature for each filling.

DO NOT DOUBLE THIS recipe for in the time it takes you to divide it and pat half of it into one pie plate or pan, the other half will cool off too much to handle without crumbling. Make each crust individually, per the recipe at the left. You can bake 2 at a time, however.

TO FREEZE THIS CRUST without a filling, partially bake it in a disposable foil pie pan on a cookie sheet, at 375F—for 12 mins. Slip the cooled pie crust in the baking pan into a plastic food storage bag. Seal it tightly and label & date it to be used within 3 months.

MY MOTHER'S PERFECT PIE CRUST

Mother's Recipe

2 cups flour
2 tsp sugar
½-tsp salt
¼-lb butter chilled & in bits
5 TB Crisco
About 5 TB cold tap water added as directed below

Combine the flour, sugar and salt in roomy bowl. Work in the butter & Crisco using pastry blender or two forks. When mixture resembles gravel, and is even in texture, you take the bowl to the sink where you will actually "drizzle" just enough cold tap water around the edge of the bowl, turning it as the water is added, to make one complete rotation — which equals about 5 TB of water. Quickly mix it only until comes away from sides of bowl. Shape into ball & cover the bowl, refrigerating it for about an hour. This rebuilds the shortening particles so that during baking they will breakdown and distribute evenly with the flour. The sugar also creates the little pockets that create "flakes" in the layers of pastry once it has been baked. After dough has chilled about an hour (or up to 3 days if you don't have time to use it right away), spread a pastry cloth out on a flat working surface. Use a rolling pin cover over your rolling pin, as well. Sprinkle some flour into the center of the cloth and smooth it over the surface. Also rub some flour into the cover on the rolling pin and working quickly, roll out the dough to about a 12" circle. Invert a greased 10" pie pan or Pyrex pie plate onto the circle. Trim away the dough, with a sharp knife, 1 inch from rim of inverted pie pan. Set the pie pan right side up and fold the circle of dough in half. Lift it carefully to fit into half of that pie pan, carefully unfolding the dough so that it fits evenly, without much "handling"! THE MORE YOU HANDLE PIE CRUST DOUGH THE LESS FLAKY IT WILL BE! "Ease" that dough into place in the pie pan. Crimp the rim. Prick the crust with tines of a fork in about 20 or 30 places. Bake at 375F—about 25 mins or till golden brown. Cool and fill with a no-bake type filling. Makes TWO 10" pie shells or ONE double crust 10" pie.

FOR THE TOP CRUST:
Gather up scraps from dough after fitting bottom crust into place. Roll out again to 10" circle. Add filling to unbaked bottom crust. Fold the 2nd circle of dough in half and place carefully over filling, unfolding the dough to ease it into place. Seal rim and cut slits in top crust for steam to escape. Wipe the top crust with Half & Half or wipe it evenly with softened butter. Bake the pie per directions for the filling you are using.

THE HOTTER THE OVEN the more your pie shell will shrink! For best results—and never mind what the other cookbooks tell you—bake a double crust pie at 375F—until crust is golden brown and the filling begins to bubble up through the slits in the top. This takes about 45 to 55 minutes, depending on the type of fruit you will be using.

SUPER QUICK GOOD

CRISCO CRUST (no rolling pin required)
6 TB Crisco   ½-tsp salt
1 TB sugar   1 cup flour
1 TB milk   Dash Cinnamon

Beat Crisco, sugar, milk, salt till creamy, adding flour in 3 or 4 portions with cinnamon, beating about a minute till very creamy. Grease 9" pie pan thoroughly or spray with Baker's Joy or Pam. With lightly floured fingers gently press dough into bottom & up sides of pan. Bake empty at 375F—20-22 minutes or till delicately browned. If you fill this with a filling that requires baking, bake the bottom crust empty at 375F—for 10 mins before adding filling. Make another recipe of the crust for the top crust, patting that portion out on Pam sprayed sheet of waxed paper to a circular diameter equal to that of the top of the pie pan you are using. Bake per filling recipe directions. This recipe makes a single 9" crust. For tart shells, allow 1½-TBspful dough per greased well. Bake tart shells empty at 375F—14-16 minutes or till golden brown. For 12 tarts.

SQUARE PAN OR ROUND PAN PEACH PIE

PEACH (Fresh) PIE
2 Recipes Crisco Crust (Partially bake one crust in 10" pie pan, per recipe directions this issue & pat out other recipe of crust to a circle 10" diameter to fit over filling later.)
The Filling:
½-cup sugar
¼-cup packed brown sugar
5 cups fresh sliced (peeled) peaches
3 TB cornstarch
½-tsp cinnamon
Dash nutmeg
Dash of Salt
4 TB butter melted
1 TB lemon juice
¼-tsp orange extract
½-cup thick peach preserves or use orange marmalade.

Combine sugars in small bowl. Put peaches into larger bowl. Combine cornstarch with cinnomon, nutmeg, salt & stir into sugars. Mix melted butter, lemon juice, extract & preserves & coat peaches well in this. Then add cornstarch mixture and coat again in this. Arrange in partially baked pie crust. Add top crust. Brush in Egg Wash. Make slits for steam to escape. Bake 350F—(lower than for the partially baked crust, remember)—30-35 mins or till crust is golden and filling bubbles up thru slits of top crust. Serve warm or cold.

Easy Way!

PEACH PRESERVES PDQ
1-lb can sliced cling peaches
2 TB cornstarch
½-tsp cinnamon
½-cup packed brown sugar
2 TB lemon juice
grated rind of 1 orange
¼-cup margarine or butter

Drain juice of peaches into a blender or jar with a tight fitting lid and add cornstarch to liquid. Blend till smooth (or put lid on jar tightly & shake the jar till mixture is smooth) —Place this in small saucepan. Cut peaches into tiny pieces. Add to cornstarch mixture with remaining ingredients & cook on med-high stirring constantly till smooth. Cool & refrigerate. Makes about 2 cups. Keeps about a month refrigerated—1 year when frozen.

I chose to work with the square pan in order to avoid working a crust up the sides and having to cut it into wedges. With the square serving pieces, the appearance is appealing and the effort in preparing the crust is as simple as buttering bread! Rather than roll out, or pat out a top crust, however, I used a second recipe of the Butter Crust for the top, without gathering it into the ball. After beating it half a minute, as the recipe always requires, I left it in the bowl, in its crumbly condition, removing the beaters, and placing the bowl in the refrigerator for 5 minutes. This hastens the firmness of the cooled crust mixture so that you can crumble it over the filling just before you bake the pie, and the final result gives you the taste and texture of the rolled out crust, with none of the effort. The filling formula remains the same in measurement and proportions, using always the 3-oz pkg of Jell-O with 1/3 cup Bisquick and 3 cans (1-lb each) drained fruit, reserving the juices & returning 1/3 of those juices to the fruit. Here are the various forumla combinations for the Square Pan Pies.

I borrowed this idea for the crumbled top crust from my very first visit to Marie Calender's Pie Shoppe Restaurants in the Los Angeles area some 7 or 8 years ago! It remains my favorite!

APPLE SQUARE PAN PIE

Prepare both crusts as directed in recipes above. Filling is made by combining 5 cups peeled, cored, thinly sliced apples, 3-oz box lemon Jell-O powder, 1/3 cup Bisquick, 2 TB bottled apple butter (or 2 TB applesauce plus 2 tsp cinnamon). Spread over hot crust at end of 15 min baking time. Crumble 2nd crust over this. Return to bake 35 min at 375F—or till apples test tender & topping is golden. Cool in pan 30 mins before cutting into squares.

BLUEBERRY SQUARE PAN PIE

The bottom crust and the crumbled top crust will be exactly as our Peach Pie Recipe recommends on the previous page. The filling, however is as follows:
- 3 cans (15-oz each) blueberries
- 3-oz box Black Raspberry Jell-O powder
- 1/3 cup Bisquick
- 1/3 cup reserved blueberry syrup
- ½-tsp cinnamon

pies the easy way!

As in the Peach Pie Recipe, prepare the 1 recipe of Butter Crust from our Index, patting it evenly over bottom of greased 9" or 8" square baking pan or Pyrex baking dish. Bake at 375F—15 mins while you prepare the filling & the topping. Drain the blueberries, catching the syrup (or juices) from these in an accomodating bowl or pan. Remove 1/3 cup to use in filling. Refrigerate the rest to use in the lovely sauce recipe I'll give you later. Mix the drained blueberries, in a bowl, with Jell-O powder, Bisquick, the reserved 1/3 cup syrup and cinnamon. Coat berries evenly in mixture & set aside. Prepare the Butter Crust again, but allow it to remain crumbled, when removing beaters, rather than gathering it into the ball as we ordinarily would for any other pie. At the end of the 15 minute baking time, spread filling over hot crust. Crumble 2nd recipe of Butter Crust over top. Return to bake at 375F—about 35 minutes or till topping appears golden brown. Cool in pan 30 mins before cutting into 9 squares or serving pieces. Refrigerate leftovers, covered, to be served within 3 or 4 days. Freezes well to be used within 90 days. Serves 6 to 8.

CHERRY SQUARE PAN PIE

- 3 cans (1-lb each) pitted, tart, red cherries
- 2 boxes (3-oz each) cherry Jell-O (not black cherry flavor!)
- ½-cup Bisquick
- ½-cup cherry liquid
- 1 tsp almond extract

While bottom Butter Crust is baking as in Blueberry Pie Recipe above, drain cherries, as for Blueberry recipe, reserving 1/2 cup this time, to compensate for the tartness of the cherries, rather than the 1/3 cup as directed in the Peach and Blueberry recipes. Mix drained cherries with Jell-O powder (using 2 boxes to allow for extra sweetness), the Bisquick and ½-cup reserved liquid plus extract. Coat cherries thoroughly. Prepare 2nd recipe of Butter Crust, as in above Pie Recipe, refrigerating till crust has baked those 1st 15 minutes. Spread filling over hot crust. Crumble crust mixture over filling. Return to bake at 375F—35 mins or till crumbled topping appears golden brown. Cool 30 mins in pan before cutting into 9 neat squares. Serves 6 to 8—allowing for 2nds! Store as in Blueberry Pie Recipe above.

"Easy as Pie"

An American original! Just after the Civil War in the devastated South, one of the few foods available was sweetened condensed milk, a new product developed in 1858. Florida cooks squeezed local Key limes to foil the canned milk's sugary-sweet taste & accidentally invented a mixture firm enough to be used as a pie filling. In its natural state, Key Lime Pie has a very pale blond color. Any green color is from a deliberate addition of food coloring. And you are free to add a few drops of green food color to the filling below if you wish.

KEY LIME PIE

- 3 eggs separated
- 14-oz can Eagle Brand Milk
- 6-oz lime juice
- 9" baked, cooled pie shell
- 6 TB sugar

Preheat oven to 425F. With mixer on med speed beat egg YOLKS with the milk till pale & frothy. Gradually beat in lime juice in thin steady stream. Pour mixture into prepared pie shell. In deep, narrow mixing bowl beat whites till frothy. Beat in sugar little at a time increasing speed till stiff & glossy. Spread over top of filling to edge of crust. Bake pie about 3 mins at 425F— just till lightly browned. Refrigerate at least 6 hours before serving to 6.

COOL WHIP POUND CAKE

- 18-oz box any flavor cake mix
- 2 cups (measured) Cool Whip
- 3 eggs
- 1¼-cups water

Blend ingredients as listed, with mixer on med speed, few minutes, scraping sides & bottom of bowl often & pour into greased/floured 10" tube pan or Bundt pan. Bake 350F— 55-60 mins or till tester inserted into center of cake comes out clean. Cool upright in pan 15 min. Invert onto a platter. Frost as desired. Serves 10.

PASTY — UPPER MICHIGAN MEAT PIE

Pronounced "pass-tease" these little meat pies were originally of Welsh or Cornish creation, brought to the upper peninsula of Michigan when copper mining was at its peak some 80 years ago or more! The miners took their meal in a pie into the mines with them, and as the stories go, which we brought back from "The Ooper", the little fold-over pies were kept warm under the miners' armpits till dinnertime in the dimly lighted mine tunnels.

The best crust for these pies, if you want to be authentic in texture and appearance is to prepare the Jiffy-brand Pie Crust Mix, right from the box, exactly as the box directs you to prepare it. The crust is not rich, and was originally made with lard, which is today an unhealthy ingredient. Chill the dough 1 hour. Then roll it out on a floured surface to ¼" thickness & use a saucer to cut out circles (about 4 from one box of the pie crust mix). Meanwhile prepare the filling:

1-lb finely ground round steak (have butcher grind it twice)!
  or use finely chopped leftover beef pot roast — 2 cupsful

1 cup grated raw rhutabaga (lg hole of vegetable grater)
1 cup finely diced raw peeled potatoes
1 large carrot, peeled & finely grated
1 onion the size of an egg - finely minced—
  or 1 TB dry minced onion
Salt & Pepper to taste

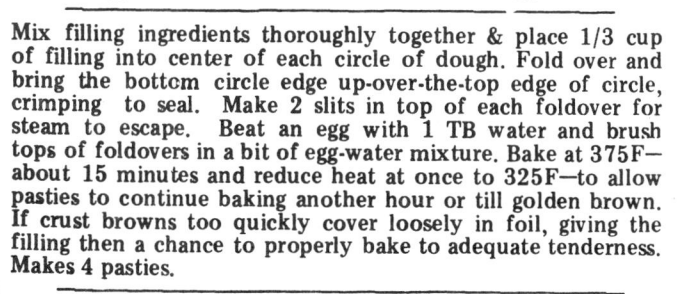

Mix filling ingredients thoroughly together & place 1/3 cup of filling into center of each circle of dough. Fold over and bring the bottom circle edge up-over-the-top edge of circle, crimping to seal. Make 2 slits in top of each foldover for steam to escape. Beat an egg with 1 TB water and brush tops of foldovers in a bit of egg-water mixture. Bake at 375F—about 15 minutes and reduce heat at once to 325F—to allow pasties to continue baking another hour or till golden brown. If crust browns too quickly cover loosely in foil, giving the filling then a chance to properly bake to adequate tenderness. Makes 4 pasties.

Prepare double crust recipe to accomodate all of filling.

Rhubarb PIE — BEST

3 TB flour
1 cup sugar
1 large beaten egg
1 cup strawberry jam
2 cups rhubarb cut into small pieces
  or 1 pint canned, drained rhubarb
9" unbaked pie shell
Whipped Cream for garnish

Combine flour and sugar. Stir egg into jam, adding sugar mixture, stirring smooth. Combine with rhubard. Spread in unbaked pie shell. Bake 425F–10 mins, reducing to 350F–for another 35 to 40 mins or till filling is "set". Cool. Chill & garnish in whipped cream. Serves 6.

MERINGUE — a little easier — ALWAYS RIGHT

3 egg whites*
Dash of salt
7-oz jar marshmallow creme or fluff

*Use whites of 3 lg eggs or 4 medium & beat with salt till foamy. Drop in the marshmallow spoonful at a time, continuing to beat, high speed, till you can remove beaters and mixture holds soft peaks. Drop the mixture by rounded spoonful over filling of pie & draw together with tip of a spatula to completely cover surface of pie. Bake at 375F— 10 to 12 mins or till golden brown.

ROMA HALL CANNOLI

Filling:
36-oz ricotta cheese
1 cup sugar
1 TB vanilla
¼-cup semi sweet chocolate chips

FOR FILLING—In Mixing bowl combine ricotta, the 1 cup sugar, vanilla. Depending on firmness of the cheese, stir or beat till smooth. Fold in chocolate chips. Cover and chill.

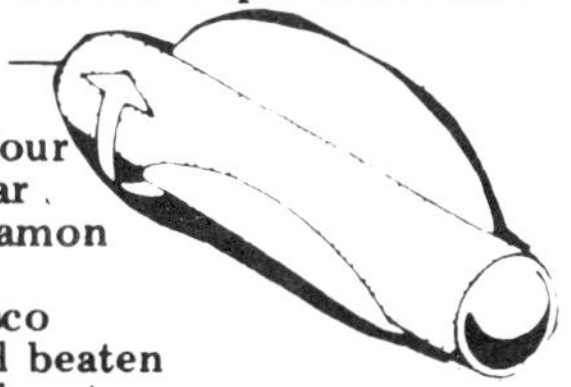

Cannoli:
2½-cups flour
¼-cup sugar
1 tsp cinnamon
¼-tsp salt
¼-cup Crisco
2 eggs well beaten
¼-cup cold water
2 TB vinegar
1 beaten egg white
1½-pint oil for deep frying
Powdered sugar

FOR CANNOLI: In large bowl, combine flour, the ¼-c sugar, the cinnamon & salt. Cut in Crisco till mixture is like small peas. In small bow, combine eggs, water, vinegar. Add to flour mixture, stirring till dough forms a ball. On lightly floured surface, roll half the dough at a time to slightly less than 1/8—in thick. Using a paper pattern & sharp knife, cut dough into ovals 6" long & 4" wide. Beginning with long side, roll each piece loosely onto cannoli tube. Seal overlapping dough with a little beaten egg white. Press gently with fingers to be sure edges are sealed. Fry cannoli in deep hot oil— (about 400F—) for 1 to 2 mins or till golden brown. Drain on paper toweling. When cool enough to handle, remove from tubes. Cool completely. About 1 hr before serving fill cannoli using pastry tube to force ricotta mixture into cones and sift powdered sugar over top. Chill. Makes about 2 dozen cannoli.

Pastry Cream

2 egg yolks
2½ tablespoons sugar
1½ tablespoons all purpose flour
½ cup milk, scalded
½ teaspoon vanilla

For cream: Combine egg yolks, sugar and flour in processor or blender and mix until smooth (or use electric mixer). Slowly beat in hot milk. Transfer to heavy nonaluminum 1- to 1½-quart saucepan and bring to simmer over medium heat, whisking constantly. Let simmer 5 minutes, whisking vigorously to prevent burning (if mixture begins to burn, remove from heat briefly and continue whisking). Transfer to mixing bowl and stir in vanilla. Cover with plastic wrap and let cool. Refrigerate. (*Can be refrigerated up to 3 days or frozen up to 2 months.*)

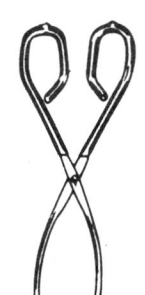

QUITE SIMPLY PIES

ANGEL PUNCH

- 2 qts Club Soda
- 1 cup Half & Half coffee cream
- 1 TB vanilla
- ½-gallon French vanilla ice cream - quite soft

Put 2 cups Club soda into blender with Half & Half, vanilla and 2 cups of ice cream. Blend till smooth. Pour into punch bowl & add remaining soda & stir in rest of ice cream. Add dash of nutmeg to each serving. (For 12) (Substitute Vernor's golden gingerale for half of Club Soda if you wish.)

CHEESECAKE CLASSIC

In the 30's & 40's cheesecake was rich, heavy and full-bodied with cheese flavor, rather than the pudding-like timid cakes of today. If you favor a substantially rich & defiantly heavy old-fashioned cheesecake, this is for you!

- ¼-lb butter or margarine, melted & warm—but not brown!
- 10-oz pkg sugar cookies, finely crushed
- 1 envelope unflavored gelatine powder

- 3 pkgs (8-oz each) cream cheese
- 1½-cups (12-oz) sour cream
- 3 TB butter or margarine—melted
- 3 TB cornstarch
- 2 large eggs
- 1 cup sugar
- 2 tsp vanilla
- dash of salt

Combine melted ¼-lb butter with cookie crumbs & gelatine powder, working together till crumbly. Remove ¼ cup mixture & set aside for topping. Grease 9" springform pan generously—or use souffle baking dish—with "straight" sides, 9" in diameter. Pat crumb mixture evenly over bottom of greased dish. Bake 350F—for exactly 8 mins. Meanwhile prepare filling by beating all remaining ingredients together, adding 1 at a time as listed above, beating well with each addition. Pour at once into hot crust at end of 8 mins-baking time. Sprinkle reserved crumbs over top. Return to bake at 350F—for 40 mins or till knife inserted 1" from edge of baking dish comes out "almost" clean. Cool in pan or baking dish on wire rack 1 hour before cutting to serve. Serves 8 easily. Keep covered & refrigerated to use in 1 week. (Freezes to be served within 6 weeks.)

CRACKER TORTE

- 6 egg whites
- ½-tsp salt
- 2 cups sugar
- 1 tsp baking powder
- 2 tsp vanilla
- 20 squares Soda Crackers or Saltine Crackers finely crushed
- 2 cups well chopped walnuts or pecans

Sundae Toppings for Fillings or Fresh Sliced Strawberries Whipped Cream or Cool Whip

Beat egg whites & salt, electric mixer, high speed till foamy. Beat in sugar little at time till stiff peaks form. Beat in baking powder & vanilla thoroughly & remove beaters. Fold in crushed crackers with rubber scraper. Fold in nuts. Divide mixture equally between 3 greased 8" or 9" round cake pans. Bake 300F—45 mins or till dry to the touch & delicately brown. Cool a few mins & loosen, removing from pans. Assemble layers with sundae topping (any flavor) spread between layers or strawberries. With palms of hands slightly apply pressure to top layer to crush a bit. Frost entire outside surface in whipped cream or Cool Whip. Chill several hours before serving 8.

SNOWY COCONUT PIE

Soften 1 envelope unflavored gelatin in ¼-cup cold water till mushy & set in heat proof cup, placed in pan of hot water till transparent. While it cools down a bit, beat 7-oz jar marshmallow creme with 8-oz carton sour cream till smooth. Beat in gelatin mixture about a minute. Remove beaters. Fold in 8-oz thawed Cool Whip, 2 tsp coconut extract & 2/3's of a 7-oz bag of flaked coconut. Pile into a prepared—or store-bought 9" chocolate crumb crust. Sprinkle remaining coconut over top, patting it down lightly with your hands. Place a large, single red Maraschino cherry smack in the center and chill it a few hours before slicing neatly to serve 6 to 8 deserving loved-ones.

HALO PIE

- 4 egg whites–reserving yolks
- ¼-tsp salt
- ½-tsp cream of tartar
- 1 cup granulated sugar
- 6-oz pkg chopped pecans

Beat 1st 3 ingredients in 1½-qt, deep-narrow bowl, high speed, about 2 mins or till soft peaks form when you remove beaters. On med speed, then add sugar a little at a time—till shiny, thick & rather stiff. Fold in pecans. Grease lightly a 10" pie pan. Spread mixture evenly into this making a well in center with sides piled about ½" to 1" higher than rim of pan. You want enough room to add filling later. Bake at 300F—about 40-45 mins or till dry & light brown. Cool while you prepare filling:

Melt 1½-squares unsweetened baking chocolate in 1½-cups milk in top of double boiler over simmering water. Whip smooth. Combine 1/3 cup sugar, 3 TB flour, dash salt & ½-tsp vanilla & beat into chocolate, continuing to cook over hot water, beating till smooth & thickened (about 10 mins). Whip yolks reserved from above meringue. Remove 1 cup of chocolate mixture, whipping into yolks just to blend & return this to remaining chocolate mixture, stirring over hot water 3 mins. Pour into pecan halo crust. Chill 1 hr before cutting into wedges to serve 6 to 8.

CHRISTMAS

ANGEL PUDDING

- 8-oz sour cream
- 8-oz carton Cool Whip
- 2 cups miniature marshmallows
- 1 cup chopped pecans
- 6-oz pkg semi-sweet chips
- 10-oz Maraschino cherries drained well & sliced
- 1 cup flaked coconut
- 4 cups bite-sized pieces Angel Food cake

Combine all ingredients as listed, stirring the 1st 2 ingredients together thoroughly and then folding in each additional ingredient. Refrigerate in covered bowl 3 or 4 hours before spooning into beer goblets, wine glasses or sherbet dishes. Top each serving with a sprinkle of chopped pecans or a dab of Cool Whip. Serves 4 to 6. Do not freeze!

French CHIFFON CHEESECAKE

Separate 3 eggs, beating the whites till foamy, adding then ½-cup sugar a little at a time, continuing to beat till stiff but not dry. Set aside. Prepare a 3¾-oz box Vanilla pudding, (not instant) by putting the required 2 cups of milk, per box directions, into blender first with the raw yolks of the eggs and blend till smooth, ½-minute. Add pudding powder & blend again till smooth. Pour into 1½-qt saucepan, cooking on med-heat, stirring constantly till thickened & smooth. Beat in 2 pkgs 8-oz each) cream cheese, in bits, & put through blender just till smooth, pouring mixture into stiffly beaten egg whites, continuing to beat on low till well combined. Pour into greased 9" souffle dish dusted in cookie crumbs—or spring form pan greased & dusted in crumbs. Chill 8 hrs before cutting to serve 8 to 10. Refrigerate leftovers 1 wk. Don't freeze!

CHEESECAKE

CAKE MIX CHEESECAKE

18-oz pkg yellow cake mix
1 egg
1/3 cup oil

2 eggs
2 pkgs (8-oz each) cream cheese
8-oz sour cream
½-cup sugar

Remove 1 cup of the dry cake mix from package and set it aside. Combine the rest of the dry cake mix right from the box, with one egg & oil. Press into bottom of greased 9x12x2" baking pan. Bake at 350F—for exactly 10 minutes. Meanwhile combine the reserved cup of cake mix with the remaining 2 eggs, cream cheese, sour cream & sugar, beating till positively smooth and creamy. At end of the 10 mins, pull rack out far enough that you can pour cream cheese mixture over hot crust and return cake to continue baking at 350F—for 35 minutes longer or till it begins to draw away from sides of pan and when you insert a knife 1" from edge of pan, it comes out clean. Cool 1 hour. Cut into squares and crown each serving with a pillow of Cool Whip & shaved chocolate candy bar. Serves 8 to 10. Keep leftovers refrigerated to be used within 3 days. Freeze to be used within 3 months.

CLASSIC DESSERT

LEGEND — LINDY'S CHEESECAKE

- 1 cup all-purpose flour
- ¼ cup sugar
- ½ cup margarine or butter, softened
- 1 egg yolk
- 1 tablespoon grated lemon peel
- 5 packages (8 ounces each) cream cheese, softened
- 1¾ cups sugar
- 3 tablespoons flour
- ¼ teaspoon salt
- 1 tablespoon grated orange peel
- 1 tablespoon grated lemon peel
- 5 eggs
- 2 egg yolks
- ¼ cup whipping cream
- ¾ cup chilled whipping cream
- 1/3 cup toasted slivered almonds

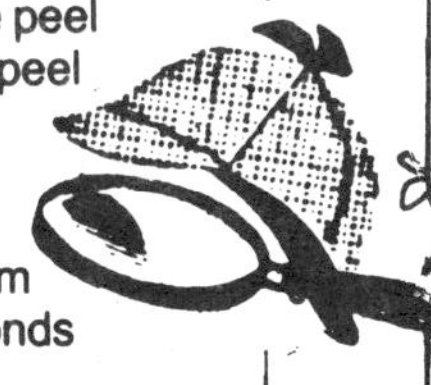

Heat oven to 400°. Grease 9-inch springform pan lightly; remove bottom. Mix 1 cup flour, ¼ cup sugar, the margarine, 1 egg yolk and 1 tablespoon lemon peel with hands. Press 1/3 of the mixture evenly on bottom of pan; place on baking sheet.

Bake until golden, 8 to 10 minutes; cool. Assemble bottom and side of pan; secure side. Press remaining mixture all the way up side of pan.

Heat oven to 475°. Beat cream cheese, 1¾ cups sugar, 3 tablespoons flour, salt, orange peel, 1 tablespoon lemon peel and 2 eggs in large mixer bowl until smooth. Continue beating, adding remaining eggs and 2 egg yolks, 1 at a time. Beat in ¼ cup whipping cream on low speed. Pour into pan.

Bake 15 minutes. Reduce oven temperature to 200°. Bake 1 hour. Turn off oven; leave cheesecake in oven 15 minutes. Cool ½ hour. Refrigerate at least 12 hours.

Loosen cheesecake from side of pan; remove side, leaving cake on bottom of pan. Beat ¾ cup whipping cream in chilled bowl until stiff. Spread whipped cream over top of cheesecake and decorate with almonds.

Ambrosia

DUFF'S STYLE PINEAPPLE CREME

Combine 16-oz sour cream, 2 cups mini marshmallows, 2 cups green grapes, 1-lb can drained pineapple chunks, 1 cup chopped walnuts or pecans & 10-oz well drained maraschino cherries with 7-oz pkg coconut and toss lightly. Chill overnight or at least 8 to 10 hours before spooning into 6 deserving dessert dishes.

CHOCOLATE MOUSSE CHEESECAKE

Beat 2 pkgs (8-oz each) cream cheese with ¼-cup sour cream till creamy and smooth. Set aside. Combine 2 boxes (3-oz each) instant chocolate pudding powder with 3 cups chocolate milk till smooth. Let stand 5 minutes to thicken & combine cheese mixture into pudding mixture, folding the two together lightly. Fill baked & cooled Patty Shells with the pudding mixture. Top each with Cool Whip and a whole, stemmed, maraschino cherry. In wine goblets, without a crust or a shell this is very, very elegant. Sufficient to accomodate 6 servings and it is best if made & chilled several hours before serving. But I wouldn't recommend freezing these.

CHILLED CHEESECAKE

3 cups cold milk
2 pkgs (8-oz each) cream cheese
2 pkgs (3¾-oz each) vanilla instant pudding powder

1 envelope unflavored gelatin
1/3 cup cold water

3¾-oz pkg chocolate instant pudding powder
1 cup milk

1 cup crushed sugar cookies in fine crumbs

Hershey's chocolate syrup

Beat the milk with cream cheese till smooth, beating in the pudding powder, and continuing to beat on high speed, till it begins to thicken. Soften gelatin in cold water. Place in micro on defrost for 1 minute till transparent, or set in pan of hot water till it clears. Beat into pudding mixture and spread evenly into greased 8" square baking dish.

Beat chocolate pudding with the 1 cup cold milk till it is smooth and spread over cheese mixture. Sprinkle cookie crumbs evenly over that and then artistically drizzle the Hershey's syrup over crumbs. Garnish further, if you wish, with chopped red maraschino cherries or chopped chocolate covered peanuts and chill 3 or 4 hours before attempting to cut it to serve 6 to 8.

THE BASICS Sensible Choice different

OLD FASHIONED FRIED FRUIT PIES

The success of this depends upon having a candy thermometer, or deep frying thermometer, which I bought at the dime store. It attaches to the side of your pan with the tip just touching the bottom of the pan, and the shortening about 3-inches deep in it, as it heats. Be sure the thermometer stands up straight. For top of the stove deep frying, use a 2½-qt heavy saucepan. I use my Revereware, copper bottom, pan on a back burner so that there is no chance of anyone touching the handle of the pan and causing an accident.

THE FRYING MIXTURE:

1 cup Safflower Oil
2 cups Crisco solid shortening
2 TB softened margarine
1 tsp light vinegar

Put it all together in the pan and begin melting the shortening on medium, heating it slowly to the 360F—mark on thermometer, at which time you can increase heat to bring it up to 380F—. Do not allow it to rise above that and regulate the temperature, by dropping a tspful of margarine into hot fat, which immediately brings the degree back down again. Also learn to adjust the temperature of the heat under the pan, using it "up" when you want to recover the temp quickly to 380F—after dropping in 2 pies at a time.

THE PIES & FILLINGS:

Use tube biscuit dough for the pie crusts. Do not use a well-known name brand because these are so much richer than the "off-brands" or house brand biscuits that they virtually fall apart while frying. Be sure you use the economical tube of biscuit dough. Open the tube & separate into the 10 biscuits it should contain. One at a time press biscuit out on waxed paper, to measure about as round as a saucer, quite thin, without letting dough have holes in it. Place 1 measuring tablespoon of thick fruit preserves or jam to one side of center of circle. Wipe the edges of half of the circle with a little beaten egg and fold circle in half, sealing well with tines of fork. If it is not properly sealed, filling oozes out while it is frying. This will cause the hot shortening to sputter and spit and make a mess, so seal them well. Do not use too much filling as it spreads and thins out when frying.

DROP ONLY TWO PIES AT A TIME into 365F— to 380F— shortening —depending on size of the pies—the larger the pie, the hotter the fat— and allow to fry 1 or 2 mins per side, giving them a nudge with tip of sharp knife to turn in hot oil mixture. Lift out with slotted spoon to drain on paper towel for ½-a-minute & quickly dip into shallow dish containing "Fried Pie Icing".

FRIED PIE ICING:

Beat together with electric mixer on high speed till smooth: ½-cup hot milk, 2 TB margarine, dash of salt, ⅓-tsp vanilla & 1-lb powdered sugar.

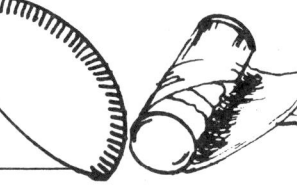

FROZEN YOGURT
Makes about 1½-quarts.

Put 4 cups yogurt into large bowl with juice of 2 lemons & rinds grated fine. Add 1 tsp vanilla, ½-cup sugar, dash nutmeg. In small deep bowl combine dash salt, 1/8-tsp cream tartar, 2 egg whites at room temperature. Beat till stiff but not dry, electric mixer, high speed. Set aside. Beat ¼-cup sugar into ½-cup heavy cream, whipping till peaks form. (I know it sounds like a lot of bowls, but trust me - it's going to be worth it!) Now carefully stir beaten egg white mixture into yogurt & then add whipped cream mixture. It will appear diluted. Don't be discouraged! Freeze till firm enough to scoop or prepare in ice cream maker according to manufacturer's directions. Makes 1½-quarts. Well drained fresh fruit may be added before freezing mixture, if desired, up to 2 cupsful.

RICE PUDDING Greek Style
Inspired by the 4-Star Restaurant (Marysville, MI) a favorite place!

We don't tell too many people about the 4-Star only because we don't want to have to stand in a line any longer than we already do when we go there 3 or 4 times a week. A traditionally Greek/American menu, I have my favorites, among which is their rice pudding, consistently good. I don't know their secret, but mine includes a little Cream of Wheat to give it body!

2 cups boiling water
1½-cups Minute Premium rice
½-cup sugar
½-tsp salt
2/3-cup very hot milk
1 tsp vanilla
2 TB butter
1 packet Mix & Eat Cream of Wheat

Combine 1st 4 ingredients in saucepan & boil hard 1 min, stirring well. Remove from heat. Cover & let stand 10 mins. Stir in milk, vanilla & butter. Sprinkle Cream of Wheat over mixture. Stir briskly to dissolve quickly. Cover again & let stand 10 min. Transfer to refrigerator container with tight fitting lid. Refrigerate overnight or several hrs to serve icy cold, dusting each serving in cinnamon. Keeps well only 2 days, refrigerated. Freeze to use in a few months. For EXTRA CREAMY mix cold rice pudding in equal parts with Cool Whip. Makes 6 servings.

BAKED CUSTARD QUICKLY

Into blender put: 3 eggs, ½-tsp nutmeg, 2½-cups milk, 1/3-cup sugar (or 1 TB liquid sweetener), dash salt, ½-tsp vanilla. Blend high speed few seconds till smooth. Pour into ungreased 9" square baking dish. Set dish in 9x12 baking pan. Add 1" water to pan. Bake as your do a custard at 350F- about 45 mins or till knife inserted in center comes out clean. Cool in baking dish in the pan 15 min. Serve warm or cold. Serves 6. If you stir 1 cup raisins into custard before baking, it's like Beef Carver Restaurant's custard.

A GREAT NEW TASTE

Gloria Pitzer's Copycat Cookbook

BEST BRAN MUFFINS

If you have ever had the high and light muffins at Dawn Donuts, you'll enjoy this quick recipe that makes up an even dozen, and with very little effort. After working with Dan Gallagher's recipe for 2 days, trying to cut it down, without losing the quality of the original result, I tried experimenting with various other ingredient combinations, using the consistency of Dan's thick, moist batter as a guide. This was a very pleasing result!

3 cups 40% Bran Flakes Cereal
1¼-cups hot milk

2 TB oil
3 eggs
½-tsp of either orange or vanilla extract

9-oz box (1-layer size) yellow cake mix

Combine cereal with hot milk in 1½-qt mixing bowl and let it stand about 10 minutes—or till cereal has absorbed all of the milk. With electric mixer on high speed, beat in the oil and eggs till completely blended. Remove the beaters. Switch to a sturdy spoon and dump in the cake mix, stirring only to moisten all of it thoroughly—but don't overmix or overbeat or muffin texture will be heavy and tough. Batter will be a bit lumpy. Cover bowl and let batter stand 15 minutes while you preheat oven to 400F—and grease 12 muffin tin wells in Crisco—evenly. Divide batter equally between the 12 wells. If you are using cupcake tin wells, you will have 15 muffins. Bake at 400F— for 20 to 25 minutes or till golden brown. Wipe tops of each while still warm in softened butter or margarine. Makes 1 dozen.

APPLE WALNUT MUFFINS

Like those served once at the famous J. L. Hudson Department Store dining rooms, you prepare the above recipe, adding ½-tsp cinnamon to the cereal when you combine it with the hot milk and then after moistening the cake mix thoroughly, you fold in 1 cup (about 2-medium sized) peeled and diced apples. Keep pieces relatively small —about as big, each, as a small pea—and then fold in ½-cup chopped walnuts. Divide batter equally between 12 muffin wells, liberally greased in Crisco. Bake at 400F—about 30 minutes or till golden brown—and tops bein to crack just a little. Makes 1 dozen. They freeze well to be used within 4 months.

ORANGE DATE MUFFINS

Like those served at the Toronto bakery shops in the underground malls—you prepare the Best Bran Muffin recipe above, using orange extract along with the eggs, as designated, and you also add the grated rind of one orange, plus 1 cup scissor-snipped dates to the cake mix when you stir that into the other ingredients. Divide batter equally between 12 Crisco coated muffin wells and bake at 400F—for 25 to 30 minutes or till golden brown and tops begin to crack slightly. Makes 1 dozen. Freeze to be used within 4 months.

BREAD PUDDING LIKE DUFF'S

Presently called "The Buffet" Restaurant in Sandusky, Ohio, Cedar Point area, this unique dessert has been requested by radio listeners and our newsletter readers for years! We often came close, but only after a dozen tests, can I now say this recipe is right on target!

1½-cups water
¾-cup nonfat dry milk powder
2 eggs
½-tsp salt (optional)
1 tsp vanilla
1 TB cinnamon

1¼-cups sugar
¼-cup margarine, melted

8 slices bread, torn into 4ths
1 cup raisins

Put all but bread & raisins into blender & blend half a minute or till thoroughly combined. Arrange bread pieces & raisins evenly in greased 9" square baking dish. Pour milk mixture over pieces & stir lightly with blade of a knife, to completely moisten all pieces of bread. Set baking dish into a 9x12x2" baking pan —not glass—adding 1" of water to pan. Bake pudding at 350F— 45 to 50 mins or till knife inserted into center comes out clean. Cool in dish in the pan of water until water is lukewarm. Add the sauce to top of pudding upon removing from oven.

SAUCE FOR BREAD PUDDING:

Into blender put 1½-cups water, 2 tsp vanilla, dash salt, ¼-cup nonfat dry milk powder, ¼-cup sugar, 2 TB cornstarch. Blend high speed half a minute or till completely smooth. Pour mixture into 1½-qt saucepan & cook, stirring constantly over med-high, about 6 to 8 minutes or till thickened and smooth. Pour over bread pudding upon removing from oven.
This recipe makes 6 to 8 servings.

THE RIGHT BALANCE

BONUS! TORONTO MUFFINS

Restaurant Style GREEK

RICE PUDDING

Another favorite restaurant has a rice pudding that is just a bit different than that of the 4-Star and developing a copycat version was not that easy. But now that it's almost on target, I can only be glad they don't have a staff of lawyers calling me to find out how I got the recipe.

3 cups milk
1½-cup COOKED long grain rice
1/4-cup uncooked MINUTE RICE (reg'l)
1/2-cup sugar
Dash salt
1 tsp vanilla
Dash cinnamon

Put all ingredients into top of large double boiler, over simmering water. Stir every 5 or 10 mins as it cooks for 1 hour or till sugar has completely dissolved & rice is tender. Be sure to replace water in bottom half of double boiler as it cooks away. Cover top pan & turn off heat. Let it stand over the hot water 1 hour. Refrigerate rice pudding in covered container several hours or overnight before serving it icy cold.
FOR CREAMIER VERSION: Mix prepared cold rice pudding in equal parts with Cool Whip. Makes 6 to 8 servings. Do not freeze please. Use within 2 or 3 days.

UNUSUAL Cookies

VARIATION:
Peanut Butter Cookies—In the recipe, substitute 3 TB creamy peanut butter for the butter or margarine. Omit O Henry Bar pieces entirely.

TURTLE COOKIES
Like the Melting Pot Shoppe sells near Grand Rapids, Michigan.

Don't be disappointed that these are not like the "traditional" turtles, for I found very little to warrant giving these cookies this name. The cookies are thick, huge, round, almost plain old-fashioned cookies like Great-Grandma might have baked.

unconventional

- 1 egg
- 1 tsp vanilla
- ½-cup sugar
- 3 TB butter (or margarine)
- 2-2/3 cups Bisquick

½-cup chopped O Henry Bars about the size of Grapenuts cereal

In medium bowl with wire whisk, whip egg, vanilla & sugar till thoroughly combined. Switch to large mixing spoon and mix in the butter with 1 cup of Bisquick till smooth. Work in rest of Bisquick, dissolving every single particle with back of the spoon. Work in the bits of O Henry Bars. Spray cookie sheet with Pam and wipe off excess with paper towel, leaving light but even coating. Divide dough into 6 equally-sized balls (each about 1/3 cup dough.) Place 2½-inches apart on prepared cookie sheet. Flatten each ball with bottom of measuring cup or drinking glass, to ½" thick circle. Do not grease the bottom of the cup or glass. Bake at 325F—for 30 to 35 mins or till lightly browned around the edges. Cool on the baking sheet 30 mins. Makes 6 gigantic cookies.

VARIETIES

WALNUT CHIP:
Prepare the same dough as given in Turtle Cookie recipe, but substitute ½-cup walnut fudge candy in crumbs about the size of Grapenuts cereal, in place of the O Henry Bar pieces. A 2-oz pkg of walnut fudge, air-dried and crumbled, is sufficient for this recipe, and these 2-oz pkgs can be found at most candy counters.

CHOCOLATE CHIP:
Prepare the same dough as given in the Turtle Cookies Recipe, however, in place of the ½-cup O Henry Bar pieces, use instead, a 6-oz pkg semi-sweet chocolate chips.

TESTED RECIPE

PEANUT BUTTER
Cookies from the dough suggested (at left) can also be used to make the Turtle Cookies, and instead of the O Henry Bar Pieces, you can use chopped chocolate covered peanuts.

CHINESE COOKIES are made from the Turtle Cookie dough in the basic recipe, adding 1 TB almond extract & ¼-cup ground almonds. Omit O Henry Bar pieces. As soon as cookies come out of oven, gently press a flat chocolate wafer candy, by Brach's, into center. Allow to cool on baking sheets 5 mins before removing to paper towels to complete cooling. Chocolate wafer candies are about as big as a quarter, sometimes with white non-parellels on the top of them.

Chinese Cookies
Fresh inspiration

BECAUSE I'M NOT A BIG FAN of the thick, not-so-sweet, old-fashioned cookie, such as the Bit O' Turtle recipe, I would instead like to recommend a Chinese Cookie that comes very close to the best I have ever sampled – These are made from our favorite "soft" cookie recipe on page 36 of our "4 INGREDIENT" book. We added almond extract to the basic dough, and then placed the flat thin chocolate candy wafer (by the Brach's people) in the center of each soon as you take it from the oven and before you remove them from the baking sheet. Here's the recipe:

CHINESE COOKIES

- ¼-cup sour cream (No substitute—use real sour cream!)
- 1 egg
- ½-cup sugar
- 1 tsp almond extract
- 2 cups Bisquick

- 1 box Brach's chocolate wafer candies
  or 3 dozen chocolate candies, each about size of a quarter

Beat sour cream together with egg & sugar & extract, using electric mixer, medium high speed, till smooth. Remove beaters & work in Bisquick till you have smooth dough, using spoon. (*)Prepare cookie sheet. Measure the dough in oval shaped measuring tablespoon, leveling it off over rim of bowl. Drop these ovals 2" apart on (*)prepared cookie sheet. Flatten each oval slightly with flat bottom of glass, greased once and dipped into sugar with each cookie flattened. Bake 400F—6 minutes exactly. Do not overbake. Soon as removed from oven, gently press chocolate candy, flat side down, into center of each warm cookie. Let cool on baking sheet 5 mins. Remove gently to continue cooling on paper towels. Cookies are very fragile while hot, but firm up nicely when cooled. Makes 3 dozen.

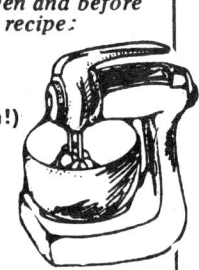

EASY MACAROONS

- 4 egg whites
- pinch of salt
- ¾ cup granulated sugar
- 1 tsp vanilla
- 2 cups shredded coconut

Preheat oven to 300F—. Lightly coat cookie sheets with Pam. Beat egg whites with salt till foamy. Gradually beat in sugar till thoroughly combined. Beat in vanilla, beating constantly till stiff but not dry. Remove beaters. Stir in coconut. Drop batter b rounded teaspoonful onto Pam-sprayed cookie sheets, about 2" apart. Bake at 300F— about 25 minutes or till delicately browned. Cool & store in air tight containers at room temperature. Makes about 5½-dozen cookies.

COCONUT MACAROONS
Combine 2-2/3 cup flaked coconut with ¾-cup of Eagle Brand Milk and 1 well-beaten egg and ¼-tsp almond extract till thoroughly mixed. Let batter stand in bowl 5 mins. Line 2 cookie sheets with brown paper. Grease paper. Drop batter 2" apart onto paper by rounded teaspoonful. Flatten each with back of spoon slightly. Bake at 325F—for 20 mins or till golden brown. Remove quickly from paper to greased plate to cool. Makes 2 dozen.

CHOCOLATE MACAROONS
Melt 4-oz bar German Sweet Chocolate over hot water & stir it into prepared batter as last ingredient. Continue as recipe otherwise directs above.

QUICK-FIX

BLANCH ALMONDS yourself & save money!

Here is the simplest way. Cover the shelled nuts in boiling water. Let stand 3 minutes. Drain well. When almonds are cool enough to handle, pinch off skins. Spread nuts on paper towel & let dry several hours. Store to use in recipes.

ALMOND CRESCENTS

½-cup finely chopped blanched almonds
1¼-cups flour
5 TB powdered sugar
¼-lb (1 stick) butter – softened
1 tsp vanilla

Blend almonds, flour & sugar. Cut in butter. Add vanilla & knead to a smooth dough. Chill 1 hour. Roll out on lightly floured board. Cut with small crescent shaped cookie cutter, placing 1" apart on ungreased baking sheet at 350F–about 10 to 12 mins or till delicately browned. (Shaping by hand into crescents–cut dough into circles ¼" thick. Cut each circle in half, drawing 2 ends toward each other on baking sheet to resemble a moon-shape.)

Quick From Scratch — MARASCHINO CHERRIES

Place two 1-lb cans sweet, red, pitted cherries & liquid in 2-qt saucepan with 2 cups sugar, the liquid reserved from a 1-lb can beets and 8-oz cherry jelly, plus a dash of salt. Bring to boil uncovered, stirring often. Reduce heat to gentle simmer. Cover and simmer about an hour, stirring every once in awhile. Cool and add two 1-oz bottles of almond extract. Keep refrigerated up to 3 months.

COOKIES

Toffee Bars

This is a crisp, thin confection that reminds you of a Heath Bar!

1 medium sized box Graham crackers
½-cup granulated sugar
1/4-lb butter or margarine
12-oz pkg semi-sweet chocolate chips
1 cup well chopped walnuts or pecans

Grease a 9x12x2" baking pan (using metal—not glass) and line with a sheet of foil on the bottom only. Arrange enough of the Graham crackers over foiled lined pan that they form a single layer, fitting snugly together. Set aside. Put sugar & butter into 1-qt saucepan & cook, stirring constantly over med-high heat till completely melted & it comes to a boil. From the first bubble of the boil, time it to boil gently 3 minutes, continuing to stir constantly. Pour boiled sugar-mixture over crackers in thin steady stream, coating the crackers evenly. Then bake the crackers at 350F—for exactly 12 minutes. Remove from oven & at once sprinkle the chocolate chips over top of hot crackers, spreading them till melted and smooth. Quickly sprinkle on the chopped nuts. Use a pizza wheel or knife while still hot, to cut into 1"x2" bars. Makes about 4 dozen. (Keep refrigerated to serve in about a week—or freeze to thaw & serve in about 3 months.)

MARY ANN STYLE OLD-FASHIONED FROSTED SPICE COOKIES

3 eggs
1 cup dark raisins
1 tsp baking soda
2 tsp apple pie spice
1 TB cinnamon
1 TB paprika
1 tsp vanilla

Put all ingredients as listed into blender. Blend on/off speed, high, about 1 minute or till raisins are so finely ground that these resemble coarse pepper. Set mixture aside. Get out your large mixing bowl, line up the following ingredients:

½-lb (2 sticks) margarine
1 cup granulated sugar
1 cup packed DARK brown sugar
"The Blender Mixture"
2 cups self-rising flour
1½-cups Quaker quick oats —used dry

On high speed with electric mixer, cream margarine till smooth, beating in both sugars till light & fluffy. Beat in "The Blender Mixture" & then the flour a little at a time till it disappears. Work in rolled oats. Prepare cookie sheet (*). Use a plastic Rubbermain ice cream scoop in which to measure dough for each cookie, or measure dough by packing it into ¼-cup measuring cup, minus 1 TB. Shape each portion pf the dough into oblong form about 2" by 4", placing these 2" apart on (*)prepared cookie sheet. Bake at 350F—exactly 12 minutes. Let cookies cool on baking sheet 5 mins. Remove carefully to complete cooling on paper towels. Makes about 3 dozen cookies. (*) See Index for Cookie sheet preparation

FROSTING—Open a 1-lb container of ready-to-spread vanilla icing. Place it in top of double boiler, over gently simmering water & stir frosting till warm and melted. Stir in 1 tsp anise extract (a licroice flavored extract). Apply this warm icing to cookies soon as you remove them from the oven and before you remove them from the cookie sheets.

ESTHER CARTER'S COCONUT CHOCOLATE CHIP COOKIES

My Mother's best cookies!

¼-lb butter
3 TB granulated sugar
9 TB packed light brown sugar
½-tsp vanilla
1 egg
½-tsp salt
½-tsp baking soda
1 cup all-purpose flour
1 cup moist flaked coconut
1 cup well chopped pecans
1 cup (6-oz) semi-sweet chocolate morsels

In medium mixing bowl, using electric mixer medium speed, beat butter till light & fluffy. Beat in both sugars till creamy. Then Beat in vanilla, egg, salt & soda. Beat 1 minute. Switch to mixing spoon, working in each remaining ingredient as listed. (*)Prepare the cookie sheet (See Index for Cookie Sheet Preparation). Drop dough by rounded measuring TB onto prepared(*) cookie sheet, 2" apart. Bake at 375F—8 minutes. Cool on baking sheet few minutes. Transfer carefully to paper towels to completely cool. Makes 3 doz.

Deluxe GOLD RUSH BROWNIES

2 cups coarsely ground graham cracker crumbs (about 20 crackers)
1 2/3 cups sweetened condensed milk
1 6-ounce package semisweet chocolate chips
½ cup coarsely chopped pecans

Preheat oven to 350°F. Lightly butter 8-inch square ovenproof glass baking dish. Line with parchment paper; butter paper. Combine all ingredients in medium bowl. Pour batter into prepared dish. Bake until lightly browned, 30 minutes. Cool in pan 10 minutes. Cut into squares. Store in airtight container.

Makes about 24

Sugar Free

STAR OF THE SHOW!
SUGAR FREE STRAWBERRY SHORTCAKE

In large mixing bowl beat together 2 cups Bisquick, 4 packets Sweet & Low, 2/3 cup skim milk, 1 egg, 1 tsp vanilla. Spread evenly over bottom of Pam-sprayed 9" square pan. Bake 350F—25 to 30 mins or till toothpick inserted in center comes out clean. Cool in pan on rack. Spread top with 1 cup sugar-free strawberry preserves. In bowl combine 20-oz sugar-free frozen strawberries, slightly thawed & 1.1-oz box strawberry sugar-free Jell-O powder. Spread over preserves. Top with 2 envelopes prepared D-Zerta Whipped Topping. Chill before serving. Cut into 9 squares. (Keep refrigerated to serve in 3 days.)

CHOCOLATE-DESSERT
SUGAR-FREE CHOCOLATE CREME

- 1-quart skim milk
- 0.3-oz box sugar-free instant chocolate pudding powder
- 0.3-oz box sugar-free instant butterscotch pudding powder
- 2½-oz pkg chopped pecans

Pour the quart of skim milk into your blender. Dump in pudding powder, used dry from the boxes. Blend high speed, on/off 2 mins or till smooth. Stop motor once or twice to scrape down sides of container. Resume blending till smooth. Divide between 6 custard cups. Sprinkle pecans over top of each. Refrigerate to serve in few days. (6 servings).

On Second Thought... a piece of cake
SUGAR-FREE FEATHERY FUDGE CAKE

The Cake:

- 1/2-tsp baking soda
- 1 cup milk
- 1/3-cup mayonnaise
- ¼-cup applesauce
- 2 TB sour cream
- 2 raw egg whites beaten till foamy
- ½-cup Nestles sugar-free chocolate QUIK powder
- 2¼-cups self-rising flour

In mixing bowl using electric mixer to combine on medium speed, beat all but last 2 ingredients well —adding 1 item at a time, beating well after each addition. Beat in QUIK till dissolves and then flour till it is smooth. Spread batter evenly into Pam-sprayed Pyrex 8½"x12x2" baking dish & bake at 350F- 25-30 mins or till tester inserted into center comes out clean. Cake will crack around edges during baking. Soon as out of the oven, let it cool on wire rack & spray top of cake evenly but lightly in Pam. Prepare topping.

SUGAR-FREE CAKE TOPPING

As box directs prepare <u>2 pkgs Cook & Serve chocolate pudding</u>. Upon removing from heat beat in <u>1 tsp liquid artificial sweetener with wire whisk (or use 4 packets dry Equal.) Spread warm pudding over warm cake.</u> Let it cool about 10 mins before cutting into 12 pieces. Refrigerate leftovers to use in a few days. Yes, it freezes well, too.====

SECRET RECIPE

SUGAR-FREE CHOCOLATE COOKIES

These are soft, slightly sweet drop cookies, that I developed, out of desperation mostly, in order to give my husband a treat that he could enjoy!

- 2 bars (2½-oz each) Estee brand milk chocolate bars
- 4 envelopes (1-serving size each) Carnation Sugar-Free Hot Cocoa Mix powder
- 1.5-oz box Sugar-Free instant chocolate pudding
- 2 cups Bisquick
- 1 cup chopped walnuts or other nuts (optional)
- 4 eggs
- 1 tsp vanilla
- 1/3 cup Crisco OIL (don't substitute melted solid shortening for this ingredient, please)
- 1 TB + 1 tsp liquid sugar subtitute (Sweet 10)

Break chocolate bars into squares & drop into your blender, blending high speed "grind"—till consistency of dry barley. Empty this into large mixing bowl & stir in cocoa mix powder, pudding powder, Bisquick & the nuts if you use them. Put remaining ingredients into blender, blending high speed, about ½-minute or till smooth & pour into chocolate mixture, using wooden or sturdy mixing spoon to combine to smooth dough. Be sure every particle of Bisquick is completely dissolved. (*)Prepare cookie sheet - see Index for Cookie Sheet Preparation. Preheat oven to 375F—. Measure dough packing it into measuring tablespoon, leveling it off over rim of bowl. Drop 1" apart on (*) prepared cookie sheet. Bake at 375F exactly 8 minutes. Cool 1 min on baking sheet. Transfer carefully to paper towels. Makes 3 dozen.

STRAWBERRY COOKIES
SUGAR FREE

These cookies are round, soft, delicately pink in color, and with attractive cracked tops that make them look exactly like bake shop cookies.

- 6 envelopes (1-serving size each) Alba '77 Fit & Frosty Strawberry Drink Mix powder
- 2 envelopes D-Zerta brand sugar-free whipped topping powder
- 2 cups Bisquick
- 4 eggs
- 1/3 cup Crisco OIL
- 2 tsp strawberry extract or vanilla
- 6 packets Sweet & Low
- 3 boxes (1-oz each) light raisins

In medium mixing bowl combine the dry drink mix powder with the whipped topping mix powder & Bisquick. Put eggs, oil, extract & Sweet & Low into blender, blending high speed for ½-minute or till completely blended. Add raisins & blend with on/off— pressing that button only 5 or 6 times "quickly" just to mince raisins. Pour blender mixture over Bisquick mixture & work well to a smooth dough, using wooden spoon or mixing spoon. Have oven preheated to 375F—and cookie sheet (*)prepared, (see Index for Cookie Sheet Preparation). Pack dough into measuring Tablespoon, leveling off over rim of bowl. Drop these ovals of dough 1" apart on (*)prepared cookie sheet. Bake at 375F—EXACTLY 8 minutes. Cool on baking sheet 2 minutes. Remove carefully to complete cooling on paper towels. Makes 3 dozen.

SUGAR-FREE EGG NOG

Into the blender put:

- 3 cups cold water
- 4-serving size instant sugar-free vanilla pudding
- 1 cup non-fat milk powder
- 1 tsp nutmeg (or less to taste)
- 4 TB sour cream (optional but it adds so much flavor!)

Blend high speed about 20 seconds and pour into 1-quart refrigerator container with tight fitting lid. Use within a week. Makes 8 punch cup servings. (Regular instant vanilla pudding can be used instead of the sugar-free for a richer eggnog.)

Gloria Pitzer's Copycat Cookbook — Pages 93 & 94

Cookies — HOW TO MAKE THEM

ARCHWAY COOKIES inspired my version here of the red spicy copycate recipe, in which the spice mixture contains ground turmeric for color and zippp!!!

RED SPICY OATMEAL COOKIES
Inspired by Archway's
And those of Little Debbie Sandwich Cookies, too. Exceptional discovery!

LITTLE DEBBIE OATMEAL CREME PIES can be imitated at home by preparing this recipe for oatmeal cookies and putting them together, sandwich style, with our Hopeless Twinkle Filling on pg 88, Fast Food Book.

Into your blender put the following:

- 3 eggs
- 1 cup dark raisins
- 1 tsp baking soda
- 1 tsp turmeric
- 1 tsp nutmeg
- 1 tsp vanilla
- 1 TB paprika
- 1 TB cinnamon

FAMOUS MAKE ALIKE COOKIES

Blend on high speed, off/on about a minute or till the raisins are so finely ground that they resemble coarse pepper. Set the mixture aside and take out your large mixing bowl & electric mixer. Assemble the following ingredients:

- ½-lb (2 sticks) margarine
- 1 cup granulated sugar
- 1 cup packed dark brown sugar
- "The Blender Mixture"
- 2 cups self-rising flour
- 1½-cups Quaker's quick oats used dry from the box

On high speed with electric mixer cream margarine till smooth, beating in both sugars till light & fluffy. Beat in "The Blender Mixture" and then the flour a little at a time till it disappears. Work in rolled oats. Prepare the cookie sheet (*). Use a plastic Rubbermaid ice cream scoop with which to measure out level scoops of dough & place 2½" apart on prepared, still warm cookie sheet. Bake at 350F— exactly 12 minutes. Let cookies cool on baking sheet 5 mins. Remove carefully to complete cooling on paper towels. Makes about 3½-dozen large cookies.

(*)Preparing the cookie sheet:
While oven is preheating to 350F—, spray cookie sheet evenly in Pam and place it empty in the 350F—oven for about 5 mins or till Pam turns brown. It is very important that you then wipe that browned Pam off with a paper towel or paper napkin so that you leave a light but even film on the cookie sheet and you do NOT have to repeat this between batches of cookies. The shortening or butter or margarine in the cookie dough will keep the baking sheet adequately greased.

Hopeless TWINKLE

COMBINE IN A LARGE MIXING BOWL:
- ¼-lb—(½-cup)—butter or margarine
- ½-cup Crisco or homogenized solid shortening
- 1 cup granulated sugar
- ¾-cup Pet or Carnation evaporated milk
- 1 TB vanilla

Cream the butter 5 mins—med speed. Add Crisco little at a time. Cream another 3 or 4 mins. A little at a time add the sugar while continue to beat. Then add the milk, mixed first with the vanilla, beating & scraping the sides & bottom of the bowl frequently. The longer you beat this the better is becomes—but food processor-preparations are also possible—timing depends on manufacturer's directions for "creaming". Mixture will actually "grow" in the bowl. Keeps refrigerated in covered container up to a month.

Chocolate Chip Cookies

The problem with most recipes is the awesome number of ingredients required. You wonder, looking at a bowl of batter, did you put in 4 cups of flour — or did the phone ring just then and was it only 3? Did you remember the salt & if you didn't, was it that important that you left it out — because somebody interrupted you at that point and your last memory of adding an ingredient was erased by the interruption! Of course, the confident cook never worries about things like that. They forge ahead brilliantly, creating cuisine that would make you and I faint at the mere thought of trying it. And even when you and I DO finally achieve a success, we're not sure it's supposed to turn out that way — that easily — because our record of near-misses, far outweigh our scores of success! The reluctant cook isn't looking for absolute perfection! We want only to create the illusion that we can cope with culinary accomplishments, riding the surfboard of certainty over the sea of success!

Fresh inspiration

If you want to make the kind of cookies at home that made Amos famous, try this version, inspired, of course, by those wonderful little lumps of goodness created by Walley Amos. My favorite version is made with the Butter Pecan Cake Mix, but in case you cannot find it where you shop, I have an alternative list of ingredients, that I am sure you c-a-n find! The method is the same for either set of ingredients. (Be sure to keep these cookies s-m-a-l-l. . .)

Famous NAMELESS CHOCOLATE CHIP COOKIES

Main	Alternate Ingredients
18-oz box Betty Crocker Butter Pecan Cake Mix	18-oz box Betty Crocker white cake mix
2 boxes (3½-oz each) instant vanilla pudding powder (used dry)	2 boxes (3½-oz each) instant butterscotch pudding (used dry)
1 cup Bisquick	1 cup Bisquick
2-oz finely ground pecans	2-oz finely ground pecans
1-2/3 cups mayonnaise	1-2/3 cups mayonnaise
12-oz semi-sweet morsels	12-oz semi-sweet morsels
2-oz chopped pecans	2-oz chopped pecans

Preheat oven to 350F—. In large mixing bowl beat together dry cake mix, dry pudding mix, Bisquick, and pecans. Work in mayonnaise to smooth, firm dough. Work in morsels and pecans. Using measuring teaspoon, shape dough into grape-sized pieces, placing 1½" apart on UNGREASED cookie sheets. Bake 350F— 15 to 16 mins. (Or till evenly golden-brown. Do not UNDER-bake these since they should be quite crisp!) Let cookies cool on baking sheets about 5 mins before removing carefully to paper towels to completely cool. Makes about 100 itsy-bitsy cookies!

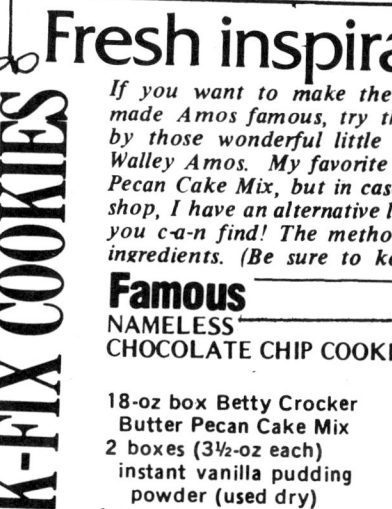

EASIER QUICK-FIX COOKIES — I FOUND A BETTER WAY

Chocolate Chip — THE ULTIMATE

Famous NAMELESS FROM-SCRATCH CHOCOLATE CHIP COOKIES

- ½-lb (2 sticks) butter or margarine
- 1 cup packed light brown sugar
- 1 cup granulated sugar
- 3 eggs
- 3 cups Bisquick
- 1 cup cornstarch
- ½-cup nonfat milk powder
- 2 TB Sanka or Coffee powder
- 1 TB unsweetened cocoa powder
- 1 TB vanilla
- 12-oz pkg semi-sweet chocolate chips
- 4-oz well chopped pecans

In large mixing bowl using electric mixer, high speed, cream butter till light & fluffy. Beat in both sugars, beating till very creamy. Beat in eggs, then each remaining ingredient, except chips and pecans. When dough is smooth, work in chips & pecans with spoon. Make grape sized pieces of dough for each cookie, placing 1" apart on ungreased baking sheet. Bake at 350F—14 mins or till golden brown. These are very crisp, so do not underbake! Makes about 12 dozen itsy bitsy cookies. Freeze baked cookies to thaw & serve in 6 months. Freeze unbaked cookie dough to thaw, shape & bake in 4 months. Recipe may be cut in half, using 2 medium sized eggs or 3 small eggs in half of a rcipe.

COCONUT MACADAMIA NUT COOKIES

Prepare the dough from recipe above, but omit chocolate chips and pecans. Instead use 4-oz well chopped Macadamia nuts. Prepare a 7-oz pkg flaked coconut by toasting on an ungreased jelly roll pan, 6" from broiler heat, stirring coconut frequently during toasting to keep it from burning. When coconut is evenly golden in color dump it onto paper covered surface to cool. Crush the toasted coconut with rolling pin or put through blender to crumbs. Then work into the dough along with Bisquick. Add Macadamia nuts as last ingredient. Continue as recipe above otherwise directs for baking.

OATMEAL RAISIN COOKIES

Prepare the dough as given in Chocolate Chip Cookie recipe above, but omit the cornstarch and instead use 1 cup of oatmeal that has been put through blender till it is consistency of flour. Measure oatmeal after blending. Place 1 cup raisins in small sieve & run cold water over raisins. Drain & dust raisins in cinnamon-sugar mixture, while still in the sieve, using 1 TB sugar to 1 tsp cinnamon. Fold the coated raisins into dough as last ingredient, along with 1 cup of walnuts instead of the chopped pecans called for in above recipe. Continue as recipe above otherwise directs for baking.

DEBBIE'S FAVORITE CHEWY BUTTERSCOTCH CHIP COOKIES
(Our daughter, Debbie, that is. . .)

The whole family enjoys these — A WHOLE NEW WAY

These are a thinner, chewy cookie, unlike the thick Mrs. Fields' very famous cookies.

- 2 cups margarine (1-pound) softened to room temperature before using.
- 1½-cups granulated sugar
- 1½-cups pkd lt brown sugar
- 2 tsp vanilla
- 4 large eggs
- 4½-cups all-purpose flour
- 2 tsp baking soda
- 2 pkgs (12-oz each) butterscotch chips

In large mixing bowl, electric mixer on med-high, cream margarine till light & fluffy. Beat in sugars a little at a time till well creamed. Beat in vanilla and eggs, beating well with each addition. Beat in only 1 cup of the flour and then beat in the baking soda till well blended. Remove the beaters and work in remaining flour with large mixing spoon till dough is smooth. Work in butterscotch morsels. Shape dough into patties, ½" thick & about 2" in diameter, using about ¼-cup dough for each cookie, placing 2" apart on (*) prepared cookie sheet. Bake at 375F only 8 minutes. DO NOT OVERBAKE or cookies will be hard when cooled. Makes about 4 dozen cookies.

PEANUT BUTTER MORSEL COOKIES—

Prepare Butterscotch Cookie Dough as directed in that recipe, but instead of 2 cups margarine, use only 1½-cups (3 sticks margarine) plus ½-cup creamy peanut butter. Use peanut butter chips instead of butterscotch. Continue as the recipe otherwise directs.

A word of advice

There's more than one way
HOW TO MAKE THEM

In my recipe books I have proven many times that you can arrive at the same result using an entirely different combination of ingredients. And recreating the cookies of our friend, Wally Amos, is a classic example. In my FAST FOOD Recipe Book I give you the original recipe as the cookies were when Wally first began to market them plus the version that we have circulated to a few million people over the years just for a self-addressed, stamped envelope.

What I urge you to remember is that I do not know what these famous food people really do put into their products, and it is more interesting not to know since it opens a number of new ways to go that depart from the traditional. Every recipe test is always a learning experience. SECRET RECIPES as Paul & I have developed them since 1973 are designed to teach our readers techniques and most of all my reasons for using the ingredients that I use. Even our daughter's favorite recipe as I give it to you here was the result of our working on coming close to Wally Amos' perfectly wonderful original cookie recipe of many years ago. The packaged product that carries his name today is the concept of the people who bought his product from him and then like many such cases, changed it just enough that it was no longer unique! Our version is a tribute to Wally.

Gloria Pitzer's Copycat Cookbook

SORTING FACTS FROM MYTHS

THE REAL STORY BEHIND MRS. FIELDS' COOKIE RECIPE!

MY FILES are filled with letters from readers of our recipes and listeners of our radio broadcasts from those who wish to share with me a cherished recipe for recreating Mrs. Fields' Chocolate Chip Cookies at home. Of course, each story is much like the one before it —as it begins with a disgruntled employee, who because he was discharged without good reason, has had access to the original recipe, and to get even, shares it with everyone he meets. Then there is the nun who wrote and asked for the recipe and received a copy along with a bill for $500 and she was advised by a lawyer to pay it. This made it then her property to do as she wished with it, and afterall, who would refuse to believe the honesty of a nun! And then there is the "member of the bar association" who requested a copy of recipe from Mrs. Fields and because no one wants to refuse a lawyer anything these day, she sent the recipe along with a bill—again—for some outrageous amount. All of these tales smack of the truth and some would be gullible enough to swallow such fabrications, but it is also a complete rerun of what occurred 30 or 40 years ago when the Waldorf Astoria Red Cake Recipe was circulating. The stories were identical and the recipe purporting to be "the original" was then shared with everyone willing to believe it's authenticity. To the wise and logical, one would know better — that the multi-million dollar company founded by Debbie Fields, now internationally based, would certainly not share the complete recipe, neither with a customer nor an employee. The complete recipe is probably known only by Debbie Fields herself. Just as with Coca-Cola, the only executives who are privileged to know the formula are not even allowed to fly on the same plane when attending meetings in distant cities from their base of operations. So do not be gullible! The original recipe, I am sure, still rests securely within the confidential files of the Debbie Fields Offices, and probably in such a coded form, that not even her most trust employee could decipher it. In the meanwhile, here is one recipe that I revamped from its original form, given to me by my good friend and neighbor, Nancy Groff. I find that the blender mixture of oatmeal and the blender chopped chocolate bar does, indeed, add exactly the right touch to make it c-l-o-s-e!

MRS. MEADOWS' CHOCOLATE CHIP COOKIES

- ½-lb (2 sticks) real butter
- 1 cup granulated sugar
- 1 cup packed light brown sugar
- 2 eggs
- 1 tsp vanilla
- ½-tsp salt
- 1 tsp baking soda
- 1 tsp baking powder

- 5 packets (1-serving-size each) Quaker Instant Oatmeal

- 2 cups all-purpose flour

- 3 bars (1.45-oz each) Nestles Milk Chocolate candy Put thru blender till like consistency & size of dry barley

- 12-oz pkg semi-sweet chocolate chips

- 1 cup chopped walnuts (optional)

Using medium sized mixing bowl and electric mixer on medium-high speed, combine first 8 ingredients, beating well with each additon. Put the 5 packets of instant oatmeal (regular flavor, please) through blender on high speed, a few seconds, till it is finely powdered, the consistency of flour. Remove beaters and work in oatmeal little at a time, and then flour, till dough is smooth. Work in ground Nestles candy and then chips & walnuts. Prepare cookie sheet (*). Measure out dough in level 1/4-cup measuring cups, shaping each into patties ½" thick and about 2" in diameter. Place 2-inches apart on prepared cookie sheets. Bake at 375F— exactly 10 minutes. Do NOT overbake or cookies will be hard when completely cool! Allow cookies to cool on baking sheet 5 minutes & then remove carefully to continue cooling on paper towels. (Thi recipe makes 2 dozen).

Cookies

MY RECIPE for Mrs. Meadows' Cookies have appeared in both my newsletters and my books since Debbie Fields famous cookies first prompted requests for a make-alike version at home. In my FAST FOOD Cookbook, on page 86 (1987 versions), you will find my recipes for the 3 best chocolate chip cookies on the market. BE CAREFUL! If you overbake the cookies they will be h-a-r-d!!! WHENEVER I receive a letter of complaint that the cookies became very hard, the cook always questions the ingredients, when actually it is the baking time that must be considered. Do NOT OVERBAKE the Mrs. Meadows' cookies.

MRS. MEADOWS' OATMEAL COOKIES

Prepare the Chocolate Chip Cookie Dough —EXCEPT you will only put 3 of the 5 packages of oatmeal into blender. Leave other 2 pkgs "as is"— emptying these into the remaining ingredients, WITHOUT blending them. Omit the chocolate chips and add instead 1 cup "plumped" raisins, plumping these by covering them in boiling water, sufficient to keep only submerged & allow to stand about 15 min or till raisins are "plump". Then drain well & blot raisins on paper towel before working into the prepared dough. Also add walnuts as directed above. (Nestles bars should also be added as in Chocolate Chip Cookie dough.) Shape and bake the cookies as directed in Chocolate Chip Cookie recipe.

RELIABLE BAKING PAN

(*)COOKIE-BAKING SHEET PREPARATION: Spray cookie sheet in Pam & place in 375F—oven, empty, 3 to 4 mins or till Pam turns brown. Wipe off brown Pam with paper towel, leaving light but even film. Drop cookies at once onto warm cookie sheet, baking per recipe directions. DO NOT REGREASE between batches of cookies. This process is good for baking 7 dozen cookies before it must be regreased.

COCONUT—MACADAMIA NUT COOKIES
Inspired by Mrs. Fields

Prepare Chocolate Chip Cookie dough per that recipe, but omit vanilla and use 1 TB coconut extract instead of the 1 tsp of vanilla! Add the Nestles candy bars as directed in the Chocolate Chip Cookie recipe, but omit chocolate chips and add instead 7-oz pkg flaked, moist coconut, that has been oven toasted on an ungreased cookie sheet, at 375F—just till delicately golden brown in color. Stir the coconut around constantly to keep color of it even and light. Cool the coconut before adding it to prepared dough. Omit walnuts and use 1 cup chopped Macadamia Nuts instead. Continue for shaping and baking as Chocolate Chip Cookie recipe otherwise directs. (Recipe makes 2 dozen).

SPECIAL EFFECT

Pillsbury said it first! And they're right! Nothin' does say lovin' like something from the oven. A real favorite of mine is a brownie recipe that can sweeten just about any relationship about to go sour because one of you must back off from a responsibility you can't handle. The offering of something you've made spells out thoughtfulness with a captial T! This is a recipe that I've worked and re-worked for weeks and weeks, trying to get it to equal, from-scratch, what Pillsbury has put into their Deluxe Brownie boxed mix. Yes, I know it would be just as simple to buy the boxed mix and forget the from-scratch, but like so many commercial products, they are eventually altered, "improved" or removed from the market entirely. It's nice to know that when you cannot get the boxed product, you have an alternative to imitating the likeness of the one you favor. I read the ingredient listings on the box & after 25 or 30 tests with various kinds of cocoa, solid chocolate and similar ingredients to those of Pillsbury, concluded that duplication would be impossible. Eventually, I worked it out and the formula was simple, much to my surprise!

Although there are two very good versions, using different types of chocolate, let me caution you, based on all of the concoctions that had to be thrown out, that semi-sweet chocolate chips will not produce an exact imitation, but the semi-sweet chocolate bars DID!

SHINY TOP BROWNIES — The Best

8-oz box Baker's semi-sweet solid chocolate
4 eggs
1-1/3 cups powdered sugar
2 tsp vanilla
1-1/3 cups Bisquick

Grease the bottom ONLY of a 9x12x2" baking pan. Melt chocolate over hot water—or in 1½-qt Pyrex mixing bowl in Micro on "Defrost". Meanwhile place the eggs in a small, deep, narrow bowl and beat on high speed with electric mixer for 3 minutes *(set your timer)!* Add the powdered sugar & beat another 3 minutes. *(Don't begrudge one second of this beating time, for this step creates the thin, sugary top on the brownie that sets this recipe apart from all others.)* Beat in vanilla for a few seconds and then scrape the mixture quickly into the bowl containing the still-warm, melted chocolate, beating to blend it quickly. At once add the biscuit mix and beat another minute or two, or till thoroughly blended. Spread batter in prepared pan, scooching every bit of batter into each corner, otherwise the brownies bake in the pan unevenly. Bake at 325F—about 30 to 35 minutes or till toothpick inserted in center comes out clean.

Cool in pan on wire rack. DO NOT use a knife to cut these or you'll mess up the shiney top. Instead run a pancake turner under cold water and insert it straight down through cooled brownies, scoring it, rather than cutting it, into neat little squares. Makes 32 pieces. Freezes well!

THE ORIGINAL—authentic recipe — **PERFECT MATCH**

Washington, D.C.
FLAGSHIP RUM BUNS

1 cup scalded milk
½ cup sugar
¼ cup shortening
1¼ teaspoons salt
1 compressed yeast cake (or substitute 1 package dried yeast)
1 egg, beaten
1½ teaspoons rum extract
3½ cups sifted flour
2 tablespoons butter, melted
¼ cup raisins, cut up

Icing:
1 cup confectioners sugar
2 tablespoons hot water
1 teaspoon rum extract

Pour scalded milk over ¼ cup sugar, shortening and salt. Cool to lukewarm, and crumble yeast into it. Beat with rotary beater until smooth. Add beaten egg and rum extract. Add ½ the flour, and beat with rotary beater until smooth. Add remaining flour and mix until smooth. Cover with a towel and let rise in a warm place (80° to 85°) until double in bulk—about 3 hours. Roll dough into two strips, each 12" long, ½" thick and 4" wide. Brush top with melted butter and sprinkle with ¼ cup sugar and raisins. Roll up, pulling dough out at edges to keep it uniform. Should be 15" long when rolled. Cut rolls in crosswise slices ¾" thick. Place in 3" greased muffin tins; cover with a towel and let rise in a warm place until double in bulk. Bake in moderately hot oven (400°) for 15 to 20 minutes. As soon as rolls are taken from oven, brush top with icing of confectioners sugar, hot water and rum extract. Makes 18 rolls.

HAWAIIAN BREAD — *marvelous*

Don't begrudge yourself the 2nd pkg of dry yeast in these recipes, where the traditional formula calls for only 1 pkg. It's the extra pkg of yeast that gives the bread that unusually light texture.

1/3 cup warm water
1 tsp sugar
2 pkgs dry yeast

1 cup milk (warm or cold)
¼-cup oil
¼-cup sugar
2 eggs
1 tsp salt
1 tsp vanilla

4¼-cups all-purpose flour

Combine 1st 3 ingredients in small cup, stirring with a toothpick. Let stand 5 mins or till doubled. In a 2½-qt mixing bowl beat remaining ingredients—except flour—till well combined. Beat in yeast mixture & work in half of flour to smooth batter. Add all but ¼-cup of flour till dough is smooth. Dip kneading hand into remaining ¼-cup flour & knead dough in bowl till no longer sticky. Cover & let rise in greased bowl, till dough doubled as in recipe at the left. Shape into loaf to fit 10" greased Pyrex Pie Plate.

Cover as in recipe at the left & let rise till doubled. Place loaf in COLD oven. Set temperature at 450F—for only 5 mins & reduce heat at once to 350F— for another 30 to 35 mins or till golden brown & crust makes hollow sound when tapped with fingers. Cool 2 hrs in pie plate before slicing. (To keep crust soft, wipe surface while bread is warm, in a TB butter or margarine.) Slice in wedges—or slice loaf in half and each half into 1" thick slices. Freezes well to use in 3 months.

Kitchen Strategies

A bread recipe caught my attention recently in a leading woman's magazine. I was about to assemble the ingredients to prepare it when I realized that the size of the pan was omitted, and in doing that I didn't know whether the pan I might select had to be greased or ungreased. Neither did the recipe give directions for how and when to remove the bread from the pan in which it was baked, whether to let it cool in the pan or on a wire rack, and for how long. All of this might seem trivial to most cooks, but when the success of a properly prepared recipe is dependent upon those small details, one is not about to guess at the omitted information, risking the loss of expensive ingredients and precious time involved in preparing it in the first place.

LET ME TELL YOU SOMETHING

about the Hot Roll Mix that may save you some time and trouble! When I was putting the ingredients together, testing the best combination for an at-home version of the store brand mix, I found that the smaller the quantity you made the easier it was to mix and blend the ingredients. If you double or triple the mix ingredients to store for 90 days or longer, per directions in the recipe, remember to also double or triple, as the case may be, the mixing time. The milk powder must be thoroughly distributed throughout the flour mixture. You can sift it or shake the mixture through a wire sieve several times or you can use a portable electric mixer on low speed to blend the dry mix ingredients. But for every 3½-cups of the mix, you will follow the yeast, water, sugar proportions as noted in the recipe.

FOR A QUICK RISE HOT ROLL mixture, in which you don't want to wait through two risings, add an extra package of yeast to the water and sugar when you prepare the rolls. You will have more of a yeast flavor in the rolls with the added package, but it will double in bulk in half the time.

HOT ROLL STICKY BUNS

Prepare the Dinner Rolls from the Hot Roll Mix as given on this page. After the last rising, shape into 12 balls. Prepare the syrup.

In small saucepan combine over medium high heat: ¼-cup sugar, 1 tsp cinnamon, 3 TB butter, 2 TB honey & 2 TB water. Stir till comes to boil. At once remove from heat. Divide equally between 12 ungreased cupcake wells. Drop the 12 balls of prepared dough into these. Let rise in warm place 45 mins or till doubled in bulk. Bake at 350F—about 30 mins or till golden brown. Cool in pan half a minute & invert into greased platter. Scrape down any excess syrup mixture and spoon over rolls. Makes 1 dozen.

SPILLS-THE-BERRIES HOT ROLL MIX

3 cups all-purpose flour
1 tsp salt
3 level TB Crisco
1 TB sugar
¼-cup dry milk powder

In medium sized mixing bowl, blend all ingredients thoroughly, using a wire whisk or a potato masher. (I prefer the whisk.) When mixture is even in texture and of very fine particles, equal almost to that of gravel, store the mixture in a well covered container and keep it at room temperature to be used within 90 days. You can keep it up to 6 months if you refrigerate it. And it keeps up to a year if you freeze it. Makes 3½-cups of mix.

TO USE THE MIX:

For Dinner Rolls:

1 envelope dry yeast
½-cup lukewarm water
1 tsp sugar
3½-cups hot roll mix
(all of the above mix recipe)

Soften yeast in warm water and stir in sugar. Let stand in a cup until it bubbles. (About 5 minutes.) Stir it into the hot roll mix and be sure that all dry particles are completely moistened in the yeast mixture. Knead it with lightly floured hands—in the bowl— until smooth and elastic in texture. You should not have to use more than 2 or 3 TB flour while kneading this dough. Place dough in greased bowl, turning dough once to grease top of it. Invert a second bowl, greased inside, over the bowl of dough and let it rise about an hour or till doubled. Punch it down and knead it 8 or 10 times in bowl. Let it rise again till doubled. Shape into 6 balls, equal in size. Place in greased muffin wells. Wipe top of each in a bit of soft butter or margarine & let rise till doubled, in warm place. Bake at 350F—about 18 to 20 mins or till golden brown. Makes 6 rolls.

Pot Pourri

Sugar Foods

SUBSTITUTE

BROWN SUGAR

Don't take this recipe lightly! You've probably heard that you can whip up a brown sugar substitute simply by adding molasses to white granulated sugar. Well, I have tried it—in every conceivable ratio and have been thoroughly disappointed! It always tasted like molasses flavored wet-sand. When you duplicate a commercial product, I believe it should be done right or not at all. Certainly the Domino people don't mix molasses and granulated sugar and put it up in boxes — so why should we settle for an inferior substitute either!

This recipe makes half a pound, which is all you should attempt to create in one batch. Do not attempt to double the recipe. If you wish to have more than the ½-pound, make it twice or 3 times or until you have as much as you need. It will keep at room temperature in a tightly covered container for months, but it keeps best and more pliable in the refrigerator — for nearly a year!

Place 1 cup granulated sugar and 2 level TB cornstarch in the blender. Cover and blend with on/off speed for 2 mins. Then blend on highest speed continuously for 5 minutes. Don't remove the cover for at least 10 minutes—or the air will fill with the sugar-dust. Letting the sugar dust settle within the blender container keeps it light and smooth. Don't be impatient & open the container one minute before that 10 minutes has expired. Set your timer!

Now place it in a bowl and work in only 1 TB dark molasses, with 1 TB also of pancake syrup (ours or bottled), using the back of a fork to mix it well. When evenly distributed return it to the blender. Cover again and blend with on/off speed on high —stopping to scrape down the sides of the container and remove the mixture from around the blade. Blend till fine and equal in consistency to commercial brown sugar.

POWDERED SUGAR

The best duplication for all practical purposes is the 1st step you must take in preparing the brown sugar recipe. Follow those directions exactly, using the 1 cup of granulated sugar & 2 level TB cornstarch with on/off speed of blender. The sugar should not be doubled. Make it up one cup at a time, guarding against removing the lid of the blender before the 10 minute settling period is up. Makes the equivilent of half a pound of commercially boxed powdered sugar.

CORN MUFFIN MIX

- 1¼-cups flour
- 1¼-cups yellow cornmeal
- 1 TB baking powder
- ½-cup sugar
- ½-cup Crisco

Combine all ingredients thoroughly, cutting in Crisco with pastry blender. Store room temperature in covered container up to 3 months.

TO USE THE MIX

- 2 cups mix
- 1 beaten egg
- ¾-cup milk
- 1 tsp vanilla

Mix ingredients well only till thoroughly moistened. Fill paper lined muffin tins half full. Bake 400 degrees 18-20 mins. Makes 1 dozen. Serve them warm.

Muffin Mix

CORN BREAD

Follow muffin preparations —but spread batter evenly in a 10" heavy iron skillet in which you have melted ¼-cup reserved bacon drippings to piping hot. Bake in skillet at 400 degrees 25-30 mins or till toothpick inserted in center comes out clean. Brush crust with melted butter & dust in sugar. Cut into pie-shaped wedges and serve warm to six.

GRAPE JUICE

GRAPE JUICE JELLY

- 2 cups bottled grape juice
- 1 cup water
- 1¾-oz pkg pectin powder
- 2½-cups sugar

In 2½-qt saucepan, combine juice, water & pectin powder on high, stirring constantly. Bring to boil. Boil 1 minute —stirring. Remove from heat. Add sugar. Stir till almost all dissolved. Return to heat. Bring back to boil. Boil ½-minute. Reduce to simmer. Simmer gently, stirring once in awhile, for 20 mins. Dip small strainer into mixture to remove foam as it forms on top of mixture. Rinse strainer under hot water, repeating this till almost all foam has been removed. Let jelly cook until it "sheets" off a metal spoon, or 2 drops on tip of spoon form 1 drop —like a syrup. Remove from heat. Cool to lukewarm. Pour into refrigerator containers & seal tightly. Refrigerate to use within 60 days. Don't freeze. Makes about 2 cups jelly.

PRESERVES

POPOVERS PROMPTLY

Into your blender, just as listed here, put each ingredient, blending well after each addition—medium speed—for about half a minute:

- 1 cup milk
- 3 eggs
- 1 TB oil
- ½-tsp salt (optional)
- 1 cup flour

Preheat oven to 450F— with muffin pans well greased or sprayed with Pam and slip the pans, empty, into oven as it preheats. Pour prepared popover batter into hot muffin wells, dividing batter equally to fill wells about 2/3's full. Bake at 450F—20 mins & at once reduce oven to 350F— to continue baking popovers about 25 to 30 mins longer or till puffy and golden brown. Make slit into top of each with tip of sharp knife & return to bake abour 2 or 3 mins longer to allow steam to escape from centers of each. Makes 6

STICKY BUNS

I make these in 2 loaf pans, freezing what will not be used in a few days. In order not to waste leftover ingredients, I use 2 loaves (1-lb each) frozen bread dough. Let it thaw until you can get a knife through it & slice each in half lengthwise. Then cut each half into 8 pieces equal in size, 32 rolls in all. Set aside. Combine a small box cook-and-serve butterscotch pudding (used dry), ½-cup firmly packed light brown sugar, 4 TB margarine, 1-tsp cinnamon, 1 cup chopped pecans till crumbly. Put just enough of mixture into each greased 9" loaf pan to thinly but evenly cover bottom of pans. Arrange 16 rolls in each pan over topping & sprinkle with remaining topping, dividing equally between the 2 pans. Cover with inverted pans of same size, greased inside, & let rise about an hour or till doubled in size. Bake in a preheated 350F-oven about 35-40 mins or till browned & bubbly. Remove from pans at once. Scrape down excess topping. Serve promptly - or cool slightly & freeze.

Do-ahead

BEST BRAN MUFFINS
Inspired by McDonald's

- 3 cups buttermilk
- 3 eggs
- 1/3-cup oil
- 1½-tsp baking soda
- 1½-tsp baking powder
- 1 tsp salt
- 1 tsp vanilla
- 1 cup sugar
- 3 cups crushed bran flakes
- 3 cups flour
- 1 cup plumped raisins *

Put 1st 7 ingredients into blender, high speed ½-minute till smooth. Pour into large mixing bowl & use mixer to beat in each remaining ingredient as listed. Do not overmix or muffins will be heavy. Cover & refrigerate batter 24 hours before using. Fill well-greased muffin wells almost full & bake 400F- 20-25 mins or till cracked on top & a toothpick inserted into centers comes out clean.*(To Plump Raisins: cover raisins with boiling water in small pan & let stand about 20 mins or till plumped. Drain well to use.)

ANOTHER TIP ON THE ADDITION OF THE RAISINS is to omit them from mixing them into the batter and instead add to the batter-filled baking tin a tablespoonful per muffin well, burying the raisins in the batter slightly. This ensures that you won't have more raisins in one muffin than you do in another. Many chefs use this method.==============

THIS BATTER keeps well refrigerated to use within 2 or 3 weeks, whether you want to bake up a dozen or just a few at a time. If you do not fill the whole tin with batter, however, be sure that you add about 1" of water to each of the empty wells. When baking the large muffins, I skip the wells, filling only every other one in a tin with batter & the others with water, so that the muffins won't bake into each other on top. You can also bake them up in greased Pyrex custard cups, placed on a cookie sheet, or in well greased & flour dusted oven-proof mugs that won't crack in the high oven heat. Just as interesting is to bake them up in tuna fish cans greased & floured & placed on a cookie sheet, adjusting the TIME, but not the temperature, to accomodate the size of the muffins.

BELGIAN WAFFLES Inspired by International House Pancakes

- 3 eggs
- 1 cup sugar
- 4 TB butter melted
- 1/4-cup cold water
- 1 tsp vanilla
- 1 cup flour
- 3/4-tsp baking powder
- 1/4-tsp salt

In medium bowl beat eggs with mixer on high speed 2 mins. Beat in sugar little at a time & then each remaining ingredient as listed, beating well after each addition. Prepare Belgian Waffle Maker per manufacturer's directions, but bake these at a slightly cooler temperature than you do basic waffles so that you have the outsides brown & crispy and the insides thoroughly baked. Dust waffle in a spoonful of powdered sugar & serve with syrup or fruit topping as desired. Makes 10

MICROWAVE Pancakes

- 2/3 cup milk
- 1 TB vinegar
- 1 TB sugar
- 1 beaten egg
- 1 cup boxed pancake mix
- 1/4-tsp vanilla

Combine milk & vinegar. Let stand 2 mins or till begins to thicken. Add sugar & egg & beat in pancake mix with spoon. Stir in vanilla. Spray 9" round Pyrex baking dish in Pam. Pour batter evenly over bottom of prepared dish and bake in Micro on "Roast" (medium) 5½-minutes. At once cover baking dish with lid or platter without removing dish from oven, but with Micro heat "off". Let it stand 3 minutes. Remove lid and cut pancake into pie-shaped wedges. Spread lightly with melted butter & dust in powdered sugar. Serve promptly drizzled in honey or syrup. Serves 4 nicely.

Cookies

THE WAFFLE IRON COOKIE
Belgian or Swedish Rosettes

Beat 2 eggs slightly, adding 2 tsp sugar & 1 cup milk in medium mixing bowl with mixer on medium speed. Add 1 cup flour & ½-tsp salt, beating till the consistency of heavy cream. Then beat in 1 tsp any flavor extract, rum, brandy flavoring or lemon or vanilla are good. Have 2 qts frying oil at 400F in a deep fryer. Dip rosette forms into hot oil to preheat them. Drain excess oil on paper towels. Next dip hot iron into batter to not more than 3/4 their depth. If only a thin layer of batter adheres to the iron, dip again till a smooth layer holds to it. Plunge the batter coated iron into the hot oil until the frequency of bubbling ceases. Remove from oil. Use fork to ease rosettes off the iron & onto paper towels to drain. Dust in powdered sugar while still warm. Makes about 6 dozen waffle rosettes.

WHEATIES MUFFINS

- ¾-cup buttermilk
- 4 TB mayonnaise
- 9-oz box (1-layer size) yellow cake mix used dry
- 1 cup slightly crushed Wheaties cereal
- ½-cup Bisquick

In 1½-qt mixing bowl, with wire whisk, whip buttermilk & mayonnaise together till well blended. Whisk in other ingredients as listed till thoroughly moistened & dissolved. Divide batter equally between SIX paper lined muffin wells. Bake at 400F—for 25 mins or till golden brown & allow to cool in pan on wire rack, 10 mins before removing to serve. Papers will remove easily when muffins are cool. Makes 6 very large muffins! Note—½-cup chopped walnuts or pecans can be added to finished batter—

BELGIUM WAFFLES

Prepare the Belgium Waffle iron per manufacturer's directions before preparing the batter.

- 2 cups flour
- 4 tsp baking powder
- 1 tsp salt
- 2 cups milk
- 4 eggs - separated
- 1 cup melted butter or oil (butter, preferred and do measure AFTER melting it).

In 2-qt mixing bowl, stir together the flour, baking powder, salt. In another smaller bowl beat the milk with the yolks of the eggs. Beat the whites till they hold their shape when beaters are removed. Stir the melted butter into the milk/egg yolk mixture. With electric mixer on medium speed, beat the milk mixture into flour mixture till smooth. With rubber bowl scraper, fold in stiffly beaten egg whites. Allow little bits of whites to remain as you fold them in. Allow about 2/3 cup batter for standard Belgium Waffle iron but use about 1/3 cup for the regular round 6" iron — or enough batter that it pours quickly and evenly over the hot, oiled iron. Bake until steaming stops or signal light on iron indicates waffle is baked. Loosen waffle with fork and lift from the iron. Reheat iron before preparing next waffle. This recipe makes about 5 waffles.

CREAM SODA HOMEMADE

Remove 1/2-cup Club Soda from a 1-qt bottle of it & either discard it or use it for something else. To the remaining soda in that bottle add 1 TB vanilla & 1/4-cup light Karo corn syrup (or for sugar-free soda, use sugar-free pancake syrup). Do not stir or shake bottle. Cap it tightly & lay it on its side in refrigerator. Turn bottle gently on its side every so often to combine ingredients & use within a weeks or so.

CINNABUNS

DURING THE EDDIE SCHWARTZ show over WGN-Chicago, Linda asked about the Cinnabuns that most malls are now offering. Here's my shortcut:

CINNABUNS

Thaw 1 loaf of frozen bread dough to the point that you can knead it lightly in a Pam-sprayed bowl. Spray your hands in a little Pam if dough is sticky, at all. Then shape dough into 1" thick ropes, coiling these around to a 6 or 7" circle, placed 2" apart on Pam sprayed jelly roll pans. You can get about 3 buns from one loaf. At the seam area of each coil, sprinkle with cinnamon-sugar (using 2 TB sugar—or Sprinkle Sweet with 1 tsp cinnamon). Drizzle top of each with Squeeze-bottle margarine or wipe in melted margarine. Let rise in warm place till doubled in size & bake at 350F—about 20 to 25 mins or till golden brown. Then soon as these are out of the oven, drizzle with Honey-Icing, made by beating together a 1-lb container Vanilla Icing and ¼-cup of honey. Serve warm. 1 loaf = 3 buns.

SUBSTITUTE

IT WAS DURING A DINNER WITH CHEF LARRY of the Muer Corporation, that Paul and I enjoyed an entree of food for thought and a very stimulating appraisal of what food should be and how it can be prepared. Chef Larry tried my sweet rolls, a recipe from which I was trying to develop a pastry dough equal to that of the Fred Sanders Company "Danish Twists"—which John Sanders told me they hadn't made for years—and even his own family wanted that recipe. With Chef Larry's helpful suggestions on how to improve my Danish, I made a few more tests and produced a fairly good likeness to the Sanders Danish Twist—but I must give appreciation to Chef Larry Pagliara of the Muer Restaurant Corporation for having put me on the right track.

DANISH PASTRY FOR TWIST Pastries

½-cup lukewarm water
2 envelopes dry yeast (4 tsp)
1 TB sugar

½-lb butter (1 cup) NOT margarine
   very soft but not melted

½-cup sugar
6 raw egg yolks (freeze the whites)
2 tsp almond extract
1 tsp vanilla
½-tsp salt
1 TB cornstarch

3 cups flour
½-cup dairy sour cream
   (Note—if you can find "pastry" flour, please use that instead of "all-purpose" flour, for a flakier texture....I used the all-purpose & it was still good but could have been "better"!)

Put the ½-cup warm water, yeast & the 1 TB sugar in 4-qt mixing bowl. Stir it a few times. Let stand 5 mins or till doubled in bulk. Cream butter in 6-cup mixing bowl, using medium speed & when light & fluffy, add sugar a bit at a time, the yolks 1 at a time, continuing to beat and scrape sides of bowl often. Add almond, vanilla, salt & cornstarch. Beat 4 minutes. Scrape this mixture into yeast mixture in larger bowl. Beat just to blend on lowest speed. Increase speed while alternately adding flour & sour cream, in about 4 portions, ending with flour. Beat 4 mins. It will be very thick. Spray insides of a Spritz Cookie Press with Pam. Fill with pastry dough. Use large hole of Spritz tips, at least ¾" in diameter and force dough onto Pam-sprayed baking sheets, 1" apart, shaping dough into the figure "8"—about 6" in length. Into each hole of the "8" figures, press 1 tsp finely crushed pecans or walnuts. Cover & let rise 1 hour. Bake at 350F—about 25 to 30 minutes or till delicately browned. At once brush each lightly with softened butter and drizzle each twist with Blender Vanilla Icing.

BLENDER VANILLA ICING:
Into your blender put: 1/3 cup warm milk, 3 TB very soft butter or margarine in bits, dash of salt, 2 tsp desired flavoring or extract and 2¾-to-3¼-cups powdered sugar, blending on high speed, scraping down the sides of container with rubber scraper, turning motor off. Scrape mixture free of blades till consistency is smooth. Additional powdered sugar may be blended into it if you wish a thicker icing. Makes 2 cups.

DANISH PAN COFFEECAKE
Prepare the dough as directed above and spread it evenly over the bottom of two 10x13x2" Pam-sprayed baking pans—at a thickness in the pan of no more than ½". Dust it evenly in cinnamon & sugar mix—see Index for this. OR buy yours in the supermarket already mixed. Then sprinkle top of each cake with raisins and chopped pecans and walnuts to your own taste. Again, then, sprinkle with cinnamon and sugar mix. Let cakes rise 30 minutes, baking one pan at a time at 350F—about 30- to 35 minutes or till dough is golden brown around edges of pan. (Lift up a corner of the cake and peek!) At once drizzle each cake with the Blender Vanilla Icing.

KENTUCKY DINNER ROLLS

THE ROLLS:

½-cup warm water
1 TB sugar
2 envelopes dry yeast

½-cup lukewarm water
½-tsp salt
2 TB oil
2½-cups flour

Combine the first ½-cup warm water with sugar & yeast in 2-qt mixing bowl. Stir 2 or 3 times. Let stand in warm place, 5 mins or till quite bubbly. Add remaining ingredients as listed, kneading in bowl with lightly floured hands, till dough is no longer sticky. Shape into a smooth ball. Place in greased 1½-qt bowl, turning dough once to grease top. Cover with another greased bowl same size, inverted over bowl of dough. Let rise 30 min in warm place. Punch down. Let rise again 30 mins. Pat out to fit bottom of greased 8" square baking dish. With tip of sharp knife, score into 9 squares. Wipe tops with a bit of soft butter or margarine. Invert another greased square baking dish, same size over rolls. Let rise till doubled, about 45 mins. Bake at 350F—about 30 mins or till golden brown. As soon as rolls are out of the oven, wipe tops with a bit more butter or margarine to keep them soft. Makes 9 rolls.

BISCUITS Inspired by Bill Knapp's

2 cups boxed biscuit mix
4 TB butter (not margarine)
1 TB sugar
½-cup buttermilk
   (not sour milk)

Egg Wash of 1 egg beaten well with 1 TB cold water

In 2-qt mixing bowl combine the biscuit mix with butter, which should be very cold & sliced into the biscuit mix in thin pieces. Sprinkle on the sugar & work into the texture of fine gravel, using a wire whisk in an up and down motion. Bear down hard on the whisk through the biscuit mixture, twisting the whisk a full turn as you do, over & over till bits of butter are barely noticed. Work in buttermilk with a sturdy spoon. Dip your kneading hand into a bit more biscuit mix only enough to knead dough in the bowl to a smooth & elastic texture. Pat it out on sheet of waxed paper to 1" thick rectangle or circle.

To cut biscuits to exact size of the original franchise biscuits, remove both ends from a 6-oz juice can. Spray inside of can in Pam or wipe well in oil. Cut out 9 biscuits, re-working scraps of dough to use it all up, shaping the last bits of dough into a patty equal in size to the others you have cut. Place close together in well greased 9" round layer cake pan. Brush tops of each biscuit in the egg wash. Try not to let egg wash touch bottom of pan or biscuits may stick when baked. Or you can dip each biscuit into the wash so that you coat only the tops and sides, being careful not to let any touch bottoms of biscuits. Bake in a preheated 450F— (very hot) oven, 20 to 22 mins or till golden brown. Makes 9 biscuits.

KENTUCKY BISCUITS

1/3 cup Club Soda
1/3 cup sour cream
1 TB sugar or 2 packets Sweet & Low
1 egg
3¼ to 3½-cups Bisquick

Mix all ingredients well in medium bowl, kneading dough in bowl, till smooth & elastic. Dip kneading hand into just enough more Bisquick dough becomes soft & smooth—not sticky and not stiff. Shape dough into 12 equal sized patties, each about 1" thick. Arrange close together on Pam-sprayed jelly roll pan. Wipe tops in dabs of soft butter or margarine. Bake at 450F—(center rack) 20 to 22 mins or till golden brown and tripled in size. Makes 1 dozen.

BEAR CLAWS

PREPARE one of my recipes for HAWAIIAN BREAD in this book... Let the dough rise in the bowl per directions in either recipe and punch it down when doubled. Then pat it out on wax paper covered surface to ¼" thickness. Cut into circles, using a one-pound coffee can from which both ends are removed. (Run a strip of masking tape around both inside rims so you won't cut your hands on any unseen jagged edges.) Spread surface of each circle of dough very lightly but evenly with melted butter or margarine. Then prepare our Struessel Mixture..(see Index)... Add 1 cup chopped pecans to that mixture if you wish. Spoon about 2 TB of mixture into center of each circle. Fold in half, pinching seams to seal. Then with Pam-sprayed kitchen scissors make a half-inch long slit, 3 times, around the folded edge, which should spread just a bit. Place on greased cookie sheets or jelly roll pans. Let rise till doubled. Bake at 375F about 30 to 35 minutes or till golden brown. At once out of the oven, drizzle each Bear Claw with a little THIN VANILLA GLAZE also in this book (see Index). Remove from baking pan to then cool on waxed paper. Makes about a dozen

Sweet Rolls

STREUSEL MIX

- 1 cup Briskquick
- 1 cup packed brown sugar
- 2 TB cinnamons-sugar mix
- 6 TB margarine in small bits

Combine it all till crumbly. Refrigerate in covered jar for 6 months. (2½-cups).

BREAD FRANKENMUTH!

HOBO YEAST BREAD

- 1/3 cup lukewarm water
- 2 TB sugar
- 2 envelopes dry yeast
- 1 tsp salt
- 1 cup 7-UP
- 2 TB oil
- 3 cups Pillsbury's Bread Flour (or use all-purpose flour)

Rinse a 3-qt mixing bowl in hot water but don't dry it. Place 1st 3 ingredients in bowl, stirring 4 or 5 times. Let stand till bubbly—about 6 to 8 minutes. Dump in salt, 7-UP & oil, stirring briefly. With spoon whip flour into this mixture, a little at a time till all of the flour is absorbed, using back of large spoon, rather than your hands. Dough will be a bit sticky—almost like a drop-type dough

Grease sheet of waxed paper. Dump dough onto this, while you wash out the mixing bowl. Dry it & spray in Pam (or wipe in oil). Smooth dough out into ball, best you can without too much handling.

Dump into that greased bowl, covering with that sheet of waxed paper, greased-side-down. Set timer for 1½-hours, leaving bowl of dough in warmish place. Go away & forget it till timer rings. With back of spoon work dough then into its original form, stirring it down well. Grease a 2½-to-3-qt oven-proof casserole dish or stainless steel bowl—preferably one with flat bottom & straight sides. Dust in cornmeal.

Shake out excess. Drop in dough. Don't spread it. Cover with a bowl of the same diameter & depth, sprayed inside. Let rise till double in bulk (about 1½-hrs). Remove top bowl. Place carefully into a COLD oven. Set temp at 450F—for only 10 mins, reducing at once to 375F—for 25 mins or till crust makes hollow sound when you tap it with your fingers.

Almost at once, remove loaf from baking dish to rest on its side on wire rack, giving loaf a quarter-turn every 15 mins for 1 hour. Then cool right side up for 2 more hrs before slicing it.

BREAKTHROUGH Sensational

HARDLY'S CINNAMON "FLAKE" BISCUITS

The Cinnamon "Flake" Mixture.

- 1-oz (1-serving size) box Kellogg's Bran Flakes
- 1 TB cinnamon
- 2 TB packed brown sugar
- 2 TB melted butter

The Biscuit Dough:

- 2½-cups Bisquick
- 2 TB granulated sugar
- ½-cup dark raisins
- 1/3 cup buttermilk
- 1/3 cup Club Soda
- ½-tsp vanilla

To prepare the "Flake Mixture empty the little box of cereal into blender. Dump in cinnamon and brown sugar & use high speed, on/off, for about 3 seconds or till crumbled, but not powdered. Empty into small bowl. Stir in melted butter with fork till mixture is completely moistened. Set aside.

To prepare biscuit dough, use a 2-qt mixing bowl. Stir Bisquick together with sugar & raisins. Put buttermilk, Club Soda and vanilla into measuring cup, without stirring and pour into Bisquick misture. Use fork to mix well till all of the liquid is absorbed. Then knead in the bowl with hands, dipping into additional Bisquick, to make dough smooth and no longer sticky. Break dough up into 4 or 5 portions in the bowl—sprinkling the "Flake" mixture over the dough and then working it into the dough with your hands till most of it is pretty well evenly distributed throughout the dough. You want more to "marblize" the dough than you do "mix" it into it. Divide dough into 12 equal parts and shape each into ½" thick patty, arranging close together in Pam sprayed 12" round or oven-proof skillet (or use two 8" round layer pans). Bake at 400F for 25 mins or till evenly golden. Remove pan to wire rack and wipe tops with icing at once using the recipe on this page.

BISCUITS Perfect

BISCUIT ICING

- 2 TB melted butter
- 1 tsp vanilla
- 2 TB sour cream
- Dash of salt
- 1½-cups powdered sugar

In small mixing bowl using electric mixer on high speed, beat all ingredients for icing till smooth. Place a rounded tablespoon of icing atop each biscuit right out of the oven. The heat of the biscuit will soften the icing just enough that you can swirl it around to coat the tops nicely, letting that icing stand on the warm biscuits half a minute before spreading it. Refrigerate any leftover icing in covered container to use within 2 weeks or freeze to use in 6 months.

EASY

HARDLY'S BUTTERMILK BISCUITS

Mix together ¼-cup 7-UP, ¼-cup buttermilk, 2 cups of Bisquick to smooth dough. Dip hand into just enough more Bisquick you can knead dough in bowl till smooth & elastic. Shape dough into 6 patties of equal size, 1" thick & place 1 patty in center of a greased 9" round layer pan. Arrange the other patties around that. Wipe tops of each in a dab of butter or margarine. Bake at 450F—(very hot oven) 18 to 20 mins or till tripled in size & golden brown. Cool in pan 10 mins before serving. Makes 6 McFabulous flaky biscuits.

FOR THE Thanksgiving CHRISTMAS HOLIDAYS

YOU CAN COPY — FESTIVE

CANDIED SWEET POTATOES

6 boiled in their jackets sweet potatoes — chilled and peeled & cut in half lengthwise
1 cup packed brown sugar
¾-tsp salt
1/3 cup butter
1/4 cup water

Arrange sweet potatoes cutside down in buttered 10" round Pyrex pie plate (or use 9" square pan well buttered). Combine the remaining ingredients in small saucepan on medium-high. Stir till sugar dissolves. Bring to boil and boil gently for 3 minutes. Let cool to lukewarm and pour over potatoes. Bake uncovered 350 oven about 50 mins basting every 10 minutes or so. Serves 6 to 8. (May be prepared several hrs ahead of serving and reheated in 400 oven 12-15 mins or in MICRO on "Simmer", dish covered with double sheets kitchen plastic wrap, 5 to 6 mins, or till bubbly.) Freeze leftovers up to 1 year.

Delicious CRANBERRY PUNCH

In punch bowl combine 1-qt cranberry juice, 1-qt prepared lemonade, 1-qt Red Pop — strawberry or cherry carbonated soda. Make ice cubes out of Red Pop also to add to punch at serving time. Add also 1-qt Sundance Brand carbonated cranberry drink or carbonated apple drink. Serves 10.

TO PREPARE CHESTNUTS

With a sharp knife cut an X on the round side of each chestnut. Spread the chestnuts in a jelly-roll pan, add ¼ cup water, and bake them in a preheated very hot oven (450° F.) for 15 minutes, or until the shells open. Remove the chestnuts and shell and peel them while they are hot.

In a skillet arrange the chestnuts in one layer. Add water to cover and simmer the chestnuts, shaking the pan occasionally, for 45 minutes, or until they are tender. Drain the chestnuts.

WASSAIL BOWL PUNCH

1 cup sugar
1/2 cup water
Lemon slices
Cinnamon sticks
4 cups red wine
2 cups cranberry-juice cocktail
2 cups lemon juice, strained

In large saucepan combine sugar, water, 3 lemon slices and 2 cinnamon sticks. Bring to boil, stirring to dissolve sugar. Boil gently 5 minutes. Strain. Combine sugar syrup, wine, cranberry cocktail and lemon juice. Heat just until hot; do not boil. Pour into serving bowl. Garnish with lemon slices. Serve hot in punch cups or mugs (each garnished with a cinnamon stick if desired). Makes eighteen 1/2-cup servings.

Frankenmuth PUMPKIN PIE

Without further ado—here is my version of "their" pie, which is one of the best commercially sold assembly-line pies I have had! At home, loving hands add what no commercial kitchen is capable of giving to somethin' from the oven.

9" Butter Crust—partially baked per that recipe (see Index) at 375F—for 16 minutes

1-lb can pumpkin
5½-oz (small size) can Pet Milk
½-cup melted butter or margarine
2 eggs
3½-oz box butterscotch pudding powder—NOT instant
1 TB pumpkin pie spice

While crust is in the oven, put the remaining ingredients together in 2-qt mixing bowl, beating with electric mixer on medium speed, about 4 to 5 minutes—or till well blended. When 16 minutes is up on crust-baking, pull oven rack out far enough that you can pour filling into hot crust and return it to bake at 375F—for 40 to 45 mins or till knife inserted in center comes out clean. Cool before cutting to serve 6.

JANET SASS'S FAMILY RECIPE FOR THE GRACE FAMILY'S BULLY PUDDING

Grease & lightly flour a 9" square pan. Place 1 cup chopped dates & ½-cup chopped walnuts in a medium sized bowl. Dust in 1 TB flour and 1 tsp baking powder. Distribute evenly in bottom of the prepared pan. In the same bowl mix together 2 slightly beaten eggs, 1 cup sugar, 1 cup milk, dash salt, ½-tsp vanilla. Pour this mixture over dates-nuts mixture. Bake at 350F—(325F if Pyrex square baking dish)—about 30 to 35 minutes or till golden brown. Cut into 9 equal squares.

This recipe has been in Janet's family since the early 1900's. Her mother's cousin brought it to Detroit from New York City, when she visited relatives here. The pudding was only served at Thanksgiving and Christmas and was named Bully Pudding because the little boys would clap their hands and shout "bully" when they saw it being brought to the table. "Bully" was the favorite expression of then-President Teddy Roosevelt. The pudding can be made ahead of time & refrigerated, covered in foil or plastic wrap, to be served at room temperature.

GRAVY (Double Boiler Style)

Remove giblets from turkey & neck from cavity. Place in 2½-quart saucepan with 7 cups water, 1 onion the size of an orange, cut into small pieces, and 4 ribs celery in 3 or 4" lengths. Bring to boil. Cover & simmer gently 1 hour. Strain, reserving liquid. Discarding the giblets (or diced to add to stuffing)—and discard celery and onion pieces. Measure enough of reserved broth that you have 28-oz, adding water to make that amount if necessary. Put liquid into blender with ½-cup Bisquick, 1 tsp poultry seasoning, 2 TB chicken bouillon powder. Pour mixture into 2-quart saucepan, cooking & stirring constantly on med-high till thickened & smooth. Pour gravy into top of double boiler & keep over hot water, about an hour prior to serving.

Sauteed mushrooms (1-lb) may be added to gravy if you like!

CRANBERRY SAUCE

Mix together a 1-lb can whole berry cranberry sauce, a 1-lb can jellied cranberry sauce and 16-oz strawberry jam. Refrigerate tightly covered to use within 30 days. Serves 6 to 8.

MAKE AHEAD MASHED POTATOES

Allow 1 large potato for each serving, peeled & in 1" cubes & cook in slightly salted boiling water just till tender to fork. Drain & mash with electric mixer, adding for each potato used, <u>1-oz cream cheese & ½-TB sour cream</u>. Salt & pepper to taste + few TB milk if needed to make creamy but not soupy. Spread mixture into shallow greased baking dish with potato mixture 2" deep. Dot with butter. Dust in paprika & seal in plastic wrap. Refrigerate up to 2 days. 1 hour before putting into oven, remove from refrigerator. Bake at 350F- 25-30 mins or till bubbly & piping hot <u>uncovered</u>.

MAKE AHEAD SKILLET STUFFING

Made & refrigerated up to 2 days before baking to serve, it takes 10 slices of crumbled bread (for 4 to 6 servings) and 14-oz can clear chicken broth, 4 TB margarine, 8-oz can of mushrooms, undrained, 2 ribs celery sliced fine, 1 tsp dry minced onion, 1 TB poultry seasoning or rubbed sage & 1 cup raisins. Stir to moisten well & heat in large skillet, stirring often medium heat 10-mins. Transfer to shallow greased baking dish. Seal in Seran Wrap. Refrigerate up to 2 days & remove from refrigerator 1 hour before baking uncovered at 350F- 25 to 30 mins or till piping hot. Serves 4 to 6.

NOTE: The 2 dishes given above can be placed in the same oven as soon as you remove the turkey from it to stand 25 - 30 mins before carving.

Spiced tea

1½-cups Tang Orange Drink Powder
1½-cups instant tea powder
1 cup lemonade powder
1 TB powdered cinnamon
1 TB cardamom powder

Decaffeinated tea is fine!

Combine it all thoroughly in a jar with a tight fitting lid, shaking the mixture, with lid tightly secured, till you can see the color and consistency is quite well distributed. TO USE: Mix 1 TB (or to taste) with 6-oz boiling water for the hot sipping drink—or use cold water and ice cubes for a refreshing change on a hot day!

HOLIDAY RECIPES
favorite holiday foods

EGG NOG — DELIGHTFULLY NON-ALCOHOLIC

In your blender combine 2 cups whole milk, 1 cup real buttermilk, 2 boxes (3½-oz each) instant French Vanilla Pudding Powder —or just instant vanilla pudding powder, 1 tsp nutmeg and blend on high speed about half a minute till smooth and creamy. Pour into punch bowl or elegant pitcher. Garnish each punch cup serving in a dusting of nutmeg. Dilute each serving with an equal amount of golden gingerale if you wish. (Do not use Canada Dry Gingerale or the eggnog may curdle!). Serves 12 nicely or 4 foolishly!

BORED ENDS EGG NOG

4 eggs - separated
14-oz can Eagle Brand Milk
Pinch of Salt (optional)
½-tsp nutmeg
1 tsp vanilla
1-oz bottle rum flavoring
1-quart milk
1-qt Vernor's gingerale

In large mixing bowl beat yolks of the eggs with electric mixer till thickened & light colored. Gradually beat in Eagle Brand Milk, salt, nutmeg, vanilla, rum flavoring and milk. In 1½-qt mixing bowl, beat whites of eggs till soft peaks form when beaters are lifted out. Fold egg whites into milk mixture. Chill several hours or overnight before serving. When you serve the eggnog, stir in the Vernor's golden gingerale (n-o-t Canada Dry Gingerale, as it is too tart & will cause eggnog to curdle!) Serve in small punch cups. Refrigerate leftover eggnog to serve within 3 or 4 days. Serves 8 adequately or 12 without seconds.

SNOW ICE CREAM — Here's the scoop

Every winter I am asked for this unique recipe that believe it or not—really does work! All you need is fresh fallen snow to complete the perfection!

13-oz can Pet or Carnation evaporated milk
1 cup granulated sugar
1 tsp vanilla extract
1 egg

Combine all ingredients as listed, beating thoroughly in medium bowl with electric mixer on high speed, adding only enough freshly fallen winter snow to mixture, that you can beat the mixture till smooth, creamy and equal in texture to a Dairy Queen Frozen Custard. Makes about 1 qt. Freeze to use within a few days.

Since birds differ in size, shape, and tenderness, use these roasting times as a general guide.

Turkey Roasting Guide

Type of Turkey	Ready-to-Cook Weight	Oven Temp.	Guide to Roasting Time
Stuffed Whole Turkey	6–8 lbs.	325°	3–3½ hrs.
	8–12 lbs.	325°	3½–4½ hrs.
	12–16 lbs.	325°	4–5 hrs.
	16–20 lbs.	325°	4½–5½ hrs.
	20–24 lbs.	325°	5–6½ hrs.
Foil-Wrapped Turkey (unstuffed)	8–10 lbs.	450°	1¼–1¾ hrs.
	10–12 lbs.	450°	1¾–2¼ hrs.
	12–16 lbs.	450°	2¼–3 hrs.
	16–20 lbs.	450°	3–3½ hrs.
	20–24 lbs.	450°	3½–4½ hrs.
Frozen Prestuffed Turkey	7–9 lbs.	325°	5–5½ hrs.
	9–11 lbs.	325°	5½–6 hrs.
	11–14 lbs.	325°	6–6½ hrs.
	14–16 lbs.	325°	6½–7 hrs.
Boneless Turkey Roast	3–4 lbs.	325°	2¼–2¾ hrs.
	4–5 lbs.	325°	2¾–3¼ hrs.
	5–6 lbs.	325°	3¼–3¾ hrs.

Servings: For turkey weighing 12 lbs. or less, allow 1 lb. per serving; over 12 lbs. allow ¾ lb. per serving.

CHRISTMAS

HOLIDAY RECIPES

MODERN MINCEMEAT

2 cups orange juice
½-cup Bisquick
1 TB apple pie spice

3 cups peeled, diced apples
2 cups raisins
16-oz can crushed pineapple, undrained

4 TB butter or margarine
1 cup finely chopped walnuts
4-serving size pkg lemon Jell-O
 (either regular or sugar-free)

Put 1st 3 ingredient into blender, high speed, for ½-minute or till smooth. Pour mixture into 2½-qt sauce, adding next 3 ingredients & cook, stirring constantly till mixture begins to thicken & become smooth (about 3 to 4 minutes). Remove from heat. Stir in butter, walnuts and Jell-O powder. Transfer mixture to greased 2½-qt baking dish. Cover with tight fitting lid & bake at 350F— 30 minutes. Remove from oven. Cool & refrigerate to use in other recipes within 30 days. Freeze to thaw & use in 6 months. Makes 8 cups mincemeat.

MINCE PIE

9" baked & cooled pie crust
4 cups prepared mincemeat
1 pint slightly sweetened
 whipped cream or topping
 (sugar-free D-Zerta whipped topping
  is suggested for sugar-free version)

Fill baked & cooled pie shell with the prepared mincemeat. Top with whipped cream or whipped topping. Garnish in a little nutmeg or cinnamon if you wish. This pie serves 6 sensibly or 2 foolishly!

HARD SAUCE
For Plum Pudding

In top of double boiler, over simmering water, combine till smooth — 1-lb container ready to spread vanilla frosting, 1 tsp almond extract, 1 tsp vanilla, ½-cup sour cream. Serve the Hard Sauce warm, spooned over each serving of Plum Pudding, or pour Hard Sauce into 8" bread loaf baking dish & chill till firm enough to cut into squares, serving each slice of Plum Pudding with a square of chilled Hard Sauce.

EGGNOG SAUCE for Plum Pudding — Prepare 4-serving size box cook-and-serve vanilla pudding as pkg directs. To finished pudding stir in ½-tsp nutmeg, 1 tsp almond extract & ½-cup sour cream. Serve sauce warm.

CASSEROLE STUFFING *Easy*

OVERNIGHT STUFFING CASSEROLE

In a greased 1½-qt baking dish mix together 1/3 cup Grapenut cereal & 6-oz box seasoned croutons (6 cups).

Put into blender till smooth:

14-oz can chicken broth
1 egg
1 tsp rubbed sage
1/3 cup applesauce

Mix into cereal-croutons & stir in 1/3 cup raisins and 1/3 cup walnuts (optional). Cover & refrigerate overnight (about 15 hours) before baking it (covered) at 350F—for 1 hr. Serves 4 to 6 nicely.

CARCASS SOUP
Leftover Turkey Stock

Take every bit of the turkey carcass with some meat on the bones yet and about 1 cup of the drippings from the pan in which you roasted the turkey & put it into a kettle large enough that you can submerge it in water with 1" above the contents. Cover it and simmer very slowly for 2 hours. Remove as many of the bones with tongs as you can and then strain out the rest. When the broth is clear, refrigerate it overnight or till all fats rise to the top and become solid. Remove the fats. Return the broth to the top of the stove and bring again to a boil. For every 18-cups of this broth you will add:

an entire stalk of celery cut up
 including the end core where all
 of the flavor is and the leaves, too—

3 white onions peeled & quartered—
 (about the size of an orange—each)

4 large carrots unpeeled & in 1" pieces

Cover & simmer on very low heat for 2 hours or till vegetables are almost mushy. Let it stand uncovered 1 hour to cool down. Then strain it and discard the vegetables. Refrigerate the broth up to a week or freeze it in family sized containers up to 6 months, adjusting the seasoning according to your taste with salt and pepper.

PLUM-GOOD

BAKED PLUM PUDDING

1-lb whole candied cherries
10-oz pkg pitted dates-cut-up
1 cup light raisins
1 cup chopped walnuts
1 TB apple pie spice
18-oz box yellow cake mix
20-oz can apple pie filling
3 large eggs
1-lb container Vanilla Icing
1-oz bottle Rum Flavoring

Save 6 cherries to use as garnish. Put the rest of them into a large mixing bowl with dates, raisins, walnuts, spice & cake mix, used dry right from the box. Mix it all well to coat fruits & nuts in the dry cake mix. Set aside and put apple pie filling into blender with eggs, blending high speed till very smooth. Pour into dry mixture. With mixing spoon combine to moisten every single dry particle in blender mixture. Pack batter into greased 9 or 10 inch Bundt or Tube pan. Bake 350F—70 mins., or till tests done. Cool in pan upright on a wire rack 1 hour. Over hot water heat frosting in small pan till it's thinned & warm. Stir in flavoring & drizzle over cake, inverted onto pretty platter. Decorate in the extra cherries. Serves 8.

ROAST TURKEY TRADITIONAL

Never mind what package directions suggest about time & temperature for roasting the bird. If you prepare it unstuffed, it will take about an hour —maybe two LESS and leave you plenty of time to finish all of the other little chores without rushing.................
Check index for our Casserole Stuffing Recipe.

Rub the cavity of the turkey with 1 TB season salt and 4 TB softened margarine. Peel 2 small onions of the papery coating & place them whole in the cavity along with two whole peeled but not cored apples...or as many of each as cavity will hold. Place the turkey directly on bottom of disposable foil roasting pan, placed on a cookie sheet to give it support. No sense having to clean that messy roasting pan when you can buy a disposable pan for a dollar in the dime store and the water, soap, energy, etc., to clean it up later would cost far more than that. Place the bird in pan on cookie sheet on lower rack of oven and set temperature at 375 degrees. Smear entire surface of bird with soft margarine—evenly but not excessively. Roast it for 30 minutes at 375. Then reduce to 350 degrees & dust entire surface of bird with 1 tsp season salt and drizzle with about ¼-cup melted butter. Let it roast this way another 30 min & then reduce heat to 325 degrees. Place a loose tent of foil over turkey & roast it 25 mins per pound—approximately. During last 30 minutes of baking time, remove foil & continue to baste every ten mins with pan drippings & additional melted butter or margarine. Dust lightly with paprika if you wish a deep mahogany colored crispy skin on the turkey. Let it stand at least 20 minutes on countertop before carving to serve. When determining how many servings —allow 1½-lbs for every serving. Roasted leftovers freeze up to 6 months.

Gloria Pitzer's Copycat Cookbook

INDEX

Almond Crescent Cookies 89
Almonds Blanched 89
Ambrosia 81
Angel Pudding 79
Angel Punch 79
Appetizer Hot Dogs 5

Apple Pie 64
Apple Pie-Caramel 63
Apples, Baked 63
Apples - Dried 62
Apples - Escalloped 63
Apple Square Pan Pie 75
Apple Walnut Muffins 86
Arthur Treacher 49
Art's Sway Red Cookies 93
Ate Once Steak Sauce 41
Bacon Oven Baked 46
Bacon Wrapped Franks 5
Baked Apples 63
Baked Beans 29
Baked Custard 84
Baked Plum Pudding 116
Banana Cake 52
Barbecued Beef 10
Barbecued Chicken 16, 17
Barbecued Ribs 13
Barbecue Sauce Dry Mix 8
Barbecue Sauce For Ribs 14
Barbecue Sauce —minutes 13
Barbecue Western 12
Bar Cake—A&P 52
Bar Cheese 40
Basic BBQ Sauce 13
Basket & Ribbons Syrup 68
Bean Salad 29
Bean Soup—US Senate 32
Bear Claws 110
Beef Barbecue 10 Brisket 36
Beef Gravy 11
Beef Roast—Rare 11
Beef Stew 35
Belgium Waffles 105
Benny Haha Dressing 43
Bill Knapp Biscuits 107

Biscuit Icing 110
Biscuit Mix Cupcakes 56
Biscuits 107
Blanching Almonds 89
Blender Gravy 11
Blender Hollandaise 33
Blender Minced Celery 6
Blender Spaghetti Sauce 20
Blueberry Sq Pan Pie 75
Blue Cheese Dressing 43
Bo Jungles Rice 33
Bran Muffins 86
Bread 109
Bread Pudding—Basic 66
Bread Pudding—Duff's 85

Brisket 36
Broccoli Quiche 18
Broccoli Soup 45
Broiling Chicken 17
Brown BBQ Sauce 13
Brownies 90
Brownies—Shiny Tops 99
Brown's Hot Fudge 69
Brown Sugar Substitute 102
Buffalo (New York) Wings 19
Bully Pudding 111

Bundt Pistachio Cake 54
Bundt Pound Cake 76
Buttermilk Dressing 43
Butter Pie Crust 72
Butterscotch Bland Puddin 59
Butterscotch Chip Cookies 98
Butterscotch 68
Butterscotch Pie Filling 58
Butterscotch Pudding Mix 58
Cajun Seasoning Mix 7
Cake Mix Cheesecake 82
Cake Mix For Cherry Cake 55
Cake Mixes
  For Yellow & Chocolate 61

Cake Top Pudding Cake 53
California Chili (No Beans) 8
Candied Sweet Potatoes 112
Candy Recipes 70, 71
Cannoli 78
Caramel Coated Apple Pie 63
Caramel Coloring Syrup 58
Caramel Icing 51
Caramels 69
Carcass Soup 115
Carrot Salad 42
Casino Sauce—Muer's 47
Casserole Lemon Cake 53
Casserole Stuffing 115
Cattleman Style BBQ Sauce 14
Cavatini 22
Celery - Blender Minced 6
Charlie's Spinach 33
Chase Sons Chili 7
Cheese 40
Cheesecake 80
Cheesecake - Lindy's 81
Cheesecake - Rich & Heavy 80
Cheese Sauce 40
Chef Garavagalia's Apple Pie 63
Cherry Nut Cake Mix 55
Cherry Pie 65
Cherry Square Pan Pie 76
Chestnuts - Roasted 112
Chicken In BBQ Sauce 12
Chicken - Basci Broiling 17
Chicken Chow Mein 19

Chicken Marinade
  Like El Pollo Loco 17
Chicken Marinated - Basic 16
Chicken Poached 16
Chicken Parmesan 20
Chicken Salad - Hudson's 15
Chicken Wings Buffalo Style 19
Chicken Soup - Frankenmuth 9

Chief Boy Hardly Dinner 24
Chiffon Cheesecake 82
Chili - Big Boy 7
Chili Cincinnati 5
Chili Con Carne 9

Chili - Lafayette 6
Chili like Chason's 7
Chili - Slow Cooker 9
Chilled Cheesecake-light 82
Chinese Cookies 87
Chinese Cookies - best recipe 88
Chocolate Cake Mix 61
Chocolate Chip Cookies-Bill's 92
Chocolate Chip Cookies
  Famous Amos Imitation 94
Chocolate Chip Cookies
  My Mom's Best Recipe 90
Chocolate Chip Turtles 87
Chocolate Cookies-no sugar 91
Chocolate Cupcakes 56
Chocolate Frosting Mix 57
Chocolate Mousse Cheesecake 81
Chocolate Pudding Mix 60
Chocolate Pudding-scratch 66
Chocolate Syrup 68
Chow Mein 19
Christmas Recipes 111-116
Chuck's Chowder 47
Church Parlor Punch 4
Cincinnati Chili 5
Cinnabuns 106
Cinnamon Flake Biscuits 110
Cinnamon Rolls 106
Coconut Macadamia
  Famous Amos 95
Coconut Macadamia
  Mrs. Meadows' Cookies 99
Coconut Macaroons 88
Coconut Pie 79
Coconut Pudding Mix 60
Coco House Dressing 43
Coffeecake 64
Coleslaw 42
Cooked Salad Dressing 44
(*)Cookie Sheet preparation 98
Cool Whip Poundcake 76
Copper Pennies Salad 42
Corned Beef Hash 36

Pages 117 & 118

Corn Muffin Mix 104
Corn Muffins 103
Cover Up Icing 67
Cracker Torte 80
Cranberry Punch 112
Cranberry Sauce 111
Cream Broccoli Soup 45
Cream Celery Soup 45
Cream Cheese Sauce 40
Cream Soda 105
Crescent Cookies 89
Cupcakes - Chocolate 56
Cupcakes - Yellow 56
Dan Gallagher's
  French Coffeecake 64
Dan Gallagher's
  Grilled Sole 35

Dan Gallagher's
  Marinade For Chicken 17

Danish Pastry 108
Debbie's Favorite Cookies 98
Deviled Ham 38
Dijon Mustard 38
Double Layer Fudge Cake 50
Dreary Queen Hot Fudge 68
Dried Apples 62
Drinks - Fizzy 48
Drunken Kinds Cake Mix 55
Dry Barbecue Sauce Mix 8
Duff's Pineapple Creme 81
Duff's Style Bread Pudding 85

Eggnog 113
Eggnog Sauce 116
Elizabeth Taylor's Dressing 43
Escalloped Apples 63
Fall Apart Beef Roast 10
Famous Nameless Cookies 94/95
Fictitious Fish 49
Fifty Seven Imitation 41
Finnan Haddie 35
Fish Batter - Treacher 49
Flagship Rum Buns 100
Floating Island 65
Fogcutter Dressing 29
Frankenmuth Bread-109 soup 9
Franks in Bacon 5
Freezer Pizza 27
French Chiffon Cheesecake 82
French Coffeecake 64
French Silk Pie 66
Fried Fruit Pies 83
Frosting - Bar Cake 52
Frosting - Fudge Cake 50
Frosting - Pistachio Cake 54
Frosting Mix - Cherry 55
Frosting Mixes 57
Frozen Yogurt 84
Fudge Cake Frosting 50
Fudge - Niagara 71
Fudge Nut Cake 50
Ginger Beer 48 /DRESSING 45
Gold Rush Brownies 90
Grape Juice Jelly 104
Grasshopper Pie 65
Gravy - Double Boiler 111
Gravy In A Pinch 18
Greek Dressing 44
Green Beans Seasoning 33
Greenfield's Bread Pudding 66
Greenfield's hot chicken salad 16
Grilled Sole 35
Groovy Gravy (Blender) 11
Gumdrops 70
Halo Pie (Meringue Pie) 79
Hangtown Fry (oysters) 31
Hard Candied - from suckers 70
Hard Cookies - to avoid them 98
Hardly's Cinnamon Biscuits 110
Hardly's Plain Biscuits 110
Hard Sauce
  For Plum Pudding 116
Hawaiian Bread 100

INDEX

High Ends Thrifty Seven....41
Hobo Bread..........109
Hollandaise..........33
Honey Baked Chicken.....19
Honey Suckle Suckers.....70
Hot Butterscotch Topping...68
Hot Chicken Salad.......16
Hot Dogs In Bacon........5
Hot Fudge - Brown's.....69
Hot Fudge - Dreary Queen..68
Hot Roll Mix.........101
Hot Roll Sticky Buns.....101
Hot Spinach Dressing.....44
Hudson's Chicken Salad...15
Hudson's Muffins.......86
Ice Box Pizza Dough.....28
Ice Cream Made With Snow.113
Italian Dinner Mix.......24
Italian Polenta........25
Janet Sass's Bully Pudding..111
Jordash Almonds........70
Kentucky Biscuits......107
Kentucky Cold Bean Salad..37
Kentucky Coleslaw......42
Key Lime Pie..........76
Lafayette Chili..........6
Lasagna - Vegetarian......21
Lasagna - Mosticiolli....25
Lasagna
   without cooking noodles..22
Latkes - Potato Pancakes...32
Lemon Beer...........48
Lemon Pudding Cake.....53
Lindy's Cheesecake.....81
Little Debbie Creme Pies...93
Liver Sausage Spread.....39
Macaroons...........88
Maid Rite Hamburgers....15
Make Ahead Chicken.....18
Make Ahead Potatoes....114
Marinade For Chicken....17
Marinade Like El Pollo...17
Marinated Carrot Salad...42
Marinated Chicken - Basic..16
Mayonnaise..........44
McFabulous Dressing.....43
Meatballs...........46
Meatloaf............46
Meatloaf Extender......39
Meat Pies - Pasties.....77
Meatsauce...........24
Melting Pot Cookies.....87
Meringue............78
Meringue Layered Torte...80
Michigan Meat Pies.....77
Microwave Pancakes....105
Mincemeat..........116

Miracle French Dressing...43
Miss Grace Cake Imitation..51
Mississippi Mud Pie.....57
Mixes For Puddings..58, 59, 60
Mix For Soup Starter....45
Molasses Taffy.........69
Mother's Best Cookies....90
Mother's Pie Crust.....73

Mrs. Fields' Story......97
Mrs. Meadows' Cookies...98
Mud Pie.............57
Muer's Casino Sauce....47
Muer's Chowder.......47
Muer's Flounder.......35
Muffins - Toronto Style..86
Muffins - Buttermilk-Bran.103
Mushroom Meat Sauce....24

Oatmeal Cookies—Meadows..98
Oatmeal Raisin Cookies...95
Olga Dressing.........44
Olga Sandwich Sauce....44
Onion Straws - Calif....23
Orange Date Muffins....86
Oven Baked Bacon......46
Oven Roasted Turkey....114
Oysters—Hangtown Fry...31
Pancakes For Micro....105
Pantry Vegetable Casserole.15
Party Cheese Sauce.....40

Pastry Cream For Cannoli..78
Pastry Danish........108
Pasty Michigan Meat Pies..77
Peach Square Pan Pie...74

Peanut Butter Turtle Cookies.87
Peas & Peanuts Salad....42
Pecan Sticky Buns.....103
Pesky Pete's Sauce......7
Pete's Sauce...........7
Pickled Ring Bologna....37
Pie Crust.........72, 73
Pies - Fried..........83
Pilaf...............34
Pineapple Creme......81
Pistachio Pudding Mix...60
Pistachio Twice Cake....54
Pizza Dough..........28
Pizza Flat Bread......28
Pizza Quiche.........27
Pizza Sauce..........27
Pizza - Skillet Style....26
Plum Pudding........116
Poaching Chicken......16
Polenta.............25
Pork Chops - BBQ.....12
Potato Pancakes......32
Pot Roast - Fall Apart...10
Pound Cake..........76
Pour Crust Cherry Pie...65
Powdered Sugar Substitute.102
Pudding Cake - Lemon...53
Pudding Mixes....58, 59, 60
Pumpkin Pie........112
Punch - Non Alcoholic..4, 79
Put Away Chicken.....18
Raisins.............70
Red Beans & Rice......33
Red Oatmeal Cookies....93
Rhubarb Pie..........77
Ribs & Kraut.........14
Rice - Cajun, Bo Jungles..33
Rice-N-Roni..........34

Rice Pilaf............34

Rice Pudding -......84, 85
Roast Beef - Pot Roast...10
Roast Beef - Prime Rib...11
Roasted Chestnuts....112
Roast Turkey Traditional..115
Roast Turkey Timetable..114
Rock Candy...........71
Roma Hall Cannoli.....78
Root Beer - Homemade..48
Rim Buns (Wash. DC)..100
Salad Dressing Cooked...44
Salami - Homemade....37
Salisbury Steak.......36
Salmon Loaf..........30
Salt Spice............41
Sanders Topping Imitation.68
Sandwich Filling......39
Saurkraut & Spareribs..14
Sausage - Homemade...38
Scampi..............30
Scrapple............46
Sham Lunchmeat......39
Shiny Top Brownies....99
Short Ribs in BBQ Sauce..14
Shrimp Burgers.......30
Shrimp On A Brick.....13
Shrimp Scampi........30
Silk Pie.............66
Sizzler Spinach.......33
Skillet Pizza.........26
Slaw - Kentucky......42
Sloppy Joes........6, 12
Slovakian Nut Candy....71
Slow Cooker Chili......9
Sneaky Pete's Sauce Info..7
Snow Ice Cream......113
Snowy Coconut Pie....79
Sole - Grilled........35
Soup Starter Mix......45
Sour Cream Hot Fudge...69
Spaghetti - How To Cook It..20
Spaghetti Pie........23
Spaghetti Sauce.....8, 24

Spaghetti Sauce
   With Cranberry Sauce...23
Spanish Bar Cake......52
Spanish Cream........65
Spanish Rice.........34
Spareribs & Saurkraut...13

Spice Cookies.........93
Spiced Tea..........113
Spinach (River Crab)....33
Spinach Salad Dressing...44
Square Pan Pie.......74
Squeeze Margarine.....40
Steak Sauce—Ate Once...41
Sticky Buns......101..103
Strawberry Cookies
   Sugar-Free..........91
Streusel Crumb Mixture.....
Stuffed Flounder......35
Stuffing Overnight...114—115
Suckers (Hudson's).....70
Sugar-Free
   Chocolate..........91
   Escalloped Apples....63
   Strawberry Shortcake..91

Swedish Meatballs.....29
Swiss Steak..........36
Tennessee Brown BBQ Sauce..13
Thanksgiving Recipes...111-116
Toffee Bar Cookies.....89
Tomato Sauce
   From Tomato Juice.....6
Tomatoes - Sugar-Free...21
Tunnel Of Love Cake....51
Turkey Roasting Chart..114
Turtle Cookies -
   Thick old-fashioned...87
Ultimate Chocolate
   Chip Cookies........92
Underwood..........38
Upper Penninsula Pasties..77
Upside Down Apple Pie..63
US Senate Bean Soup....32
Vanilla Frosting Mix....57
Vanilla Pudding Mix....59
Vegetable Casserole - Pantry.15
Vegetarian Chili.......31
Vegetarian Lasagna....21
Velveeta Fudge........71
Velveeta Stretcher.....40
Walnut Chip Cookies....87
Wassail Bowl........112
Watergate Cake.......67

Wheaties Muffins.....106
White Baked Beans (KY)..37
Wilted Lettuce........44
Wing Dings..........19
Yogurt - Frozen.......84
Yogurt Sauce (Olga)....44
Yellow Cake Mix......61
Yellow Cupcakes.......56

Prices of our books are subject to change without notice so if the date on the cover of this book is more than a year ago, it's best to write to us for a current price list and what books are still available. We are constantly adding new books to our list and revising others. Use the address on the cover of this book to inquire about ordering from us or check with Books In Print at your local library.